Damn!

Reflections on Life's Biggest Regrets

Damn!

Reflections on Life's Biggest Regrets

K.C. & Ron,

You won't regret it!

Barry Cadish

Barry Cadish 505·636·3969

**Andrews McMeel
Publishing**

Kansas City

01 02 03 04 05 RDC 10 9 8 7 6 5 4 3 2 1

Library of Congress Cataloging-in-Publication Data
Cadish, Barry.
 Damn! : reflections on life's biggest regrets / Barry Cadish.
     p. cm.
 ISBN 0-7407-0762-0 (pbk.)
   1. Conduct of life. 2. Regret. I. Title.

BJ1548 .C33 2001
081—dc21   00-046427

Book design by Holly Camerlinck

To everyone who trusted a stranger in cyberspace—
and had the courage to confide.

Contents

Acknowledgments

Without the support and encouragement of many people along the way, this book—or any book, for that matter—would have been impossible to write. Most likely, it would be just an idea, sitting in a drawer somewhere.

These are some of the friends, family, and colleagues who kept me motivated. My heartfelt gratitude goes to:

Michel Gregory, who was my lunch companion on that serendipitous December day when the idea was first conceived. Thanks for not laughing—and for picking up the check.

John Moss, who suggested I create a Web site in the first place and who never doubted the concept. Period. Thanks for keeping me abreast of many Internet-related opportunities.

Meloney Chadwick, who never tired of hearing about this project, *repeatedly,* whenever we'd get together. Thanks for your enthusiasm, advice, good humor, and for always lending an ear.

Sam Meddis, who somehow found my press release and listed my Web site on USATODAY.com—directly below *The Blair Witch Project.* (That must mean something; I just don't know what.) Thanks for getting things rolling.

Betsy Wolfenden, cofounder and president of Restitution Incorporated, who sent me Harvey's powerful letter. Thanks for opening a small window into the prison system and letting me peek inside.

Rex Black, Lorene Cary, Lionel Fisher, Sam Horn, Eric Kimmel, Mike Lynberg, and "Sophia," authors themselves, who provided valuable insights into the publishing industry. Thanks to all of you for jump-starting my career.

My agent, Stacey Glick, who found me after reading a newspaper article about RegretsOnly.com. Thanks for your patience, your guidance, and for helping me develop a winning proposal.

My editor, Jean Zevnik, who actually *bought* my proposal just three weeks after it was submitted. Thanks for taking a chance and for letting me become the writer I've always wanted to be.

My parents, Jerry and Arlene, who always thought I had it in me, whatever *it* is. Thank you for your boundless love and for finally sending me your responses. (Sorry I didn't use yours, Mom.)

My brothers, Rick and Todd, who never seemed to mind my jabbering about the book, by phone, one thousand miles away. Thanks for your feedback and for having faith in your big brother.

My wife, Melissa, and my daughters, Michelle and Hilary, for not being *too* upset when, for months, I hogged the computer. I love you all and I regret not saying it enough. Thanks for enduring more than your fair share.

The many anonymous individuals around the world (participants and nonparticipants alike) for their comments and good wishes. Thanks for believing in me. Your kind words were always a great source of inspiration.

Anyone who ever inquired, "How's the book going?" Thank you for caring enough to ask.

Finally, special recognition goes to Jim Hier, my dear friend and talented Webmaster who guided me onto the World Wide Web. He talked me out of doing things I wanted to do; he talked me into doing things I *didn't* want to do. And his instincts were always correct. The countless nights and weekends he sacrificed for me—instead of being with his family—were invaluable. Thank you for your dedication and for being a sounding board on just about everything. I always said I couldn't do it without you, Jim. Now, everyone else knows it, too.

**Whatever you can do, or dream you can, begin it.
Boldness has genius, power, and magic in it.**

—Goethe

Introduction

I will never forget the day my life changed: December 18, 1998. It was a Friday, exactly twenty days before President William Jefferson Clinton's impeachment trial began. That afternoon, I was meeting a friend for lunch and my first thought was, "What the *heck* will we talk about?" I had known Michel for only two months. I was a writer/producer with the NBC television affiliate in Portland; she was one of my clients. Although we collaborated on a few local public service commercials, I was still nervous about making conversation.

With the impeachment trial looming, President Clinton and Monica Lewinsky were on the tips of everyone's tongues. I figured they would be ideal subjects to help me break the ice. I wondered aloud if Mr. Clinton really regretted his affair with Miss Lewinsky or was it something else? Sure, he regretted getting *caught,* but if I could ask the President about the biggest regret of his life, what would he say? And if Monica herself wasn't at the pinnacle of the President's regrets, then what—or who—might it be?

My natural inquisitiveness didn't stop there. I finally said to Michel, "Wouldn't it be fascinating to find out what people's biggest regrets are?" I also suggested how revealing it might be to compile them into a book someday—comparing people's regrets on a variety of life experiences.

After all, regrets are universal; nearly everyone has them. Regrets transcend age, gender, race, culture, nationality, religion, language, social status, and geographic location. Imagine what we could learn by sharing our stories, our choices, and even our regrets.

Michel agreed and before we knew it ... lunch was served. We talked about little else, and the name—Regrets Only—seemed to jump right out.

When Michel and I departed, I promised myself I would complete an outline of the concept by the end of January. I let the idea stew for several weeks, and then wrote this rough draft that I wanted desperately to share:

Dear _____,

I'm contacting people, via e-mail, and asking them only this: "What is your biggest regret in life?" Or, put another way, "What would you do differently if you had another chance?" In either case, it can be anything in life you regretted doing or perhaps something you didn't do, but wish you had. . . .

The most illuminating responses will be compiled into a book that I hope to publish someday. The length of your "regret" doesn't matter. It can be serious or humorous, in whatever style pleases you. My idea sprang from all the craziness in Washington these days, as well as the rest of the world. I thought it would be fascinating to explore our collective psyches to see what we could learn from life's choices—and from each other.

Still interested? If so, you should dig deep within yourself and write with more openness and more sincerity than you've ever expressed. . . . Please use your real first name, not your Internet user name. (You can put "Name withheld" on your submission if it allows you to write more candidly.)

The way I see it, everyone has a story to tell and I'd like to hear yours. . . . However, if you choose not to participate, that's OK. All I ask is that you e-mail this request to your friends and relatives. Beyond that, there's nothing more I can add.

Thank you very much for giving this some consideration. You won't regret it.

As a former advertising copywriter, I had created thousands of concepts during my twenty-year career, but *never* had an idea taken hold of me like this one. I wanted feedback right away, so that evening I showed it to my wife, Melissa, who is one of the sweetest, most thoughtful, most caring, and most upbeat people on the *planet*. Melissa was in bed, reading. She paused from her magazine and read the "letter" as I stood there, silently, and watched. Then, somewhat nonchalantly, she looked up and said, "You always see the glass as half-empty, instead of half-full."

While her reaction disappointed me, I knew instantly that I had a crucial decision to make: I could answer, "Yeah, maybe you're right. Maybe it's not such a great idea, after all" and crumpled up the paper, never mentioning it again. Or, I could go against my wife's judgment and just e-mail the letter anyway. I halfheartedly thanked her for her comments, walked into my home office, sat at the computer, cut and pasted the regrets letter into my message window, entered various e-mail addresses, hit "send"—and let 'er fly.

◆ ◆ ◆

Feedback came almost immediately. My sister-in-law, Linda, considered it a "chain letter" and refused to pass it on. A few friends thought it was a joke; a few more thought I was crazy. Others were intrigued enough to want to know if it really *was* a joke and/or if I really *had* gone crazy.

But eight days after that e-mail, Tony and his wife, Henrietta— a couple I had never met—sent the first actual submission:

Our biggest regret in life (we are blessed and have few) is not being able to be more tolerant of other people's shortcomings.

Now, this wasn't exactly the font of inspiration I had hoped for, but it was a good start, nevertheless. I was encouraged by the candor of their response, but I was seeking greater depth and far more introspection. The next day, I got exactly what I was looking for: a brief, poignant account of a thirty-four-year-old man's struggle against alcoholism. As painful as his story was, I felt it might lead other people to recognize their own demons and, perhaps, inspire them to confront their addictions or other difficulties they faced.

Within days of these first two submissions, more regrets trickled in—all from strangers. Original recipients who liked the idea were obviously forwarding my request to their friends, relatives, and colleagues. People were sending candid, heartfelt, and thought-provoking responses. Some were even humorous.

I knew I was onto something, but didn't realize just how significant it would be until a couple months later when I ran into my friend John, who suggested I create a Web site to obtain regrets from around the world.

Since I could barely navigate my way through Windows 98, let alone design and implement a Web site, I turned to another close friend, Jim. He had launched his own genealogy Web site, as a hobby, two years earlier and agreed to help. For the next two months, we worked tirelessly on the project.

From the outset, this was going to be a copy-intensive Web site. And with so many poorly conceived Web sites already out there, I wanted mine to surpass every vertigo-inducing design I had seen. Jim and I debated strategies, typefaces, logos, graphics, colors, layouts, and overall tone. The Web site would have no sound, no flashing/spinning/scrolling icons, and no psychedelic backgrounds. Also absent were monkeys, gophers, or any other critters to "click on" in order to win a prize. In fact, there would be no extraneous elements to distract people from deep reflection—or from thoughtful writing.

The key, however, was making the Web site completely anonymous. If this site was, indeed, a place for serious contemplation about our choices in life—and people were willing to be completely honest—then it had to be a comfortable place for them to *write* honestly. That's why I requested only a person's first name, age, and occupation. For added privacy, one could simply put "Name withheld." More importantly, on the actual regret submission form, I could *never* see anyone's e-mail address unless they typed it themselves.

Finally, I made a conscious—and risky—decision not to include or accept any advertising. To me, a Web site cluttered with annoying ads would destroy the idea and compromise the original intent of the project: namely, using the Internet as a research tool to gather anonymous regrets for a book. It would live or die via word-of-mouth and by whatever publicity I could generate on my own.

◆ ◆ ◆

On April 27, 1999, RegretsOnly.com made its debut. And for the rest of that month, a whopping eleven people logged on to the Web site. Some were friends or relatives; the remaining "visitors" were actually me, just checking to see if the darn site was still functioning. It was.

In May, 418 logged on; June brought 1,459 more. Then, on July 30, 1999, I struck gold: RegretsOnly.com was listed as a USATODAY Hot Site after I sent them a press release. Suddenly, my site was swamped with visitors. In what seemed like a matter of hours, other Web sites around the country and throughout the world had already linked RegretsOnly.com to theirs. (Any doubts I had about the speed or impact of the Internet were quickly erased.)

RegretsOnly.com was getting international exposure. Visitors logged on from Australia, Belgium, Brazil, Canada,

Denmark, England, Germany, Greece, India, Ireland, Italy, Japan, Malaysia, the Netherlands, New Zealand, Norway, Pakistan, Portugal, Scotland, Singapore, Sweden, and Thailand. Even folks in the Russian Federation and the Czech Republic checked out the Web site.

More important than the international appeal was the variety of responses from people in all walks of life. Replies came from teachers, lawyers, administrators, factory workers, secretaries, business owners, journalists, nurses, bankers, homemakers, teenagers, seniors, war veterans, and former prison inmates. They wrote about childhood, love, marriage, sexuality, education, careers, children, grandparents, money, pets, addictions, and crime.

These unsolicited respondents were more frank and sincere than I had ever imagined. People participated because RegretsOnly.com is a safe and comfortable forum in which to write truthfully, especially behind a cloak of anonymity—and they were genuinely intrigued by the concept.

What's more, I didn't belittle or berate anyone, nor did I pass judgment. I didn't wag the proverbial index finger in their faces, telling them they did a bad thing. I am not a psychologist, therapist, counselor, or new-age guru. And, I'm not Dear Abby or Ann Landers, so I don't give advice.

Basically, I'm just an average person who put forth a simple idea: that by writing candidly about our regrets and openly sharing them, we can inspire each other to make better choices.

Even today, after nearly two thousand responses, there are more people who are grateful for the opportunity to share their thoughts. Words such as "cathartic" and "therapeutic" are used frequently, with many respondents saying they want others to learn from their experiences.

Some folks have compared RegretsOnly.com to a confessional, but that's inaccurate as well as misleading. A confessional signifies religion and there's nothing religious about it. A confessional also suggests "sinful" behavior, but most of the regrets included here could hardly be called sinful. Finally, a confessional implies forgiveness and since I'm not a priest or rabbi, there's nothing for me to forgive. Besides, people have already lived their regrets; they can write from experience about a subject that has been on their minds—and is close to their hearts.

No matter what people say, the regrets collected here are more than just by-products of a so-called online confessional. As one respondent named Dianna pointed out: *"In a confessional, you're all alone with a sometimes judgmental priest, whereas at your Web site, you can read how human and vulnerable we all are and not just a bunch of awful, hell-bound sinners— just people who sometimes make wrong choices."*

♦ ♦ ♦

Life's choices. That's *exactly* what this book is about, seen from the inside out. Now, you must decide what each regret means to you and then apply what you have learned to your own life.

Before you start, there are a few things you should know: aside from correcting obvious spelling, punctuation, and grammatical errors, I did minimal editing. Every participant's capitalized or italicized words, quotation marks, and parenthetical comments are their own.

Since most of us tend to write the way we talk, each submission should sound as if that person were speaking directly to you. So rather than "Americanizing" everything, I allowed for cultural differences and left certain words intact. In fact, I wanted to make sure the 290 distinct voices you hear are *theirs*, not mine. My comments, plus any words added for clarity are in brackets [ ].

As I mentioned, all contributors had the option of providing an e-mail address. If they did and the address was phony, their submission was automatically discarded. Because if they weren't truthful about their e-mail address, I couldn't very well trust their story.

After you read these regrets, anecdotes, and observations, three things may happen: first, you will appreciate your own situation and, most likely, not take so much for granted. Second, you will identify with one or more of the participants and should be motivated to make positive changes in your life before embarking on the same path. And third, you will discover you are not alone in the choices you have made.

Finally, one small caveat: If you are seeking a scholarly "How-to" book, with step-by-step instructions promising to change your life overnight, you won't find it here. But if you favor more provocative and insightful material that will challenge your thinking like never before, *Damn!* is for you.

This book is for anyone who wants to probe his/her life in fresh and enlightening ways. *Damn!* is deeply personal, sometimes dark, and, yet, always honest. It offers wisdom, thoughtfulness, and common sense from real people around the world.

With heartfelt words, the gutsy individuals within these pages convey the drama, conflicts, humor, frustrations, tragedies, hopes, dreams—and hard realities—of everyday life.

So, if you truly are not afraid of an occasional jolt to your psyche, then please read on:

You won't regret it.

chapter 1

Just You and Me, Babe

'Tis better to have loved and lost
Than never to have loved at all.

—Alfred, Lord Tennyson

No other subject generated as much interest as relationships, with women outnumbering men by more than two to one. Why? The simple answer is that on nearly every topic covered in this book, women submitted far more regrets than men. Overall, women accounted for about 60 percent of the regrets I received.

The better answer, however, is that women, for the most part, are able to talk more willingly and openly about what they want in a relationship. And being able to "talk" anonymously makes their task even easier.

Men were no less passionate or emotional about their relationships; they just contributed fewer opinions on the subject. Some of them—as well as some women—simply wanted to vent.

Fortunately, no matter what people regret in the areas of romance and companionship, they never regret their kids. Having kids, regardless of the circumstances, seems to add dimension to a person's life and, when all else fails, lends perspective to one's relationship that might otherwise be lost.

The regrets in this section fall into several categories: first, there's the ever-popular, centuries-old mystery involving love. That includes first love, lost love, too much love, not enough love, and looking for love in all the wrong places. It's a subject that continues to confuse and confound people of all ages as they try to balance the need for companionship with the search for the perfect companion.

Companionship often means romance, and romance usually leads to marriage: many regrets centered around couples who tried—and failed—to keep their marriages together and those who are hanging on, for better or worse. Naturally, they regret the time spent with the wrong mate. It's just too bad they didn't discover it sooner.

There are also people who yearn for familial soul mates. Here's where introspection and reflection abound as people try to build new relationships and savor existing ones. Whether in making new friends or just getting to know their families a little better, people still want to connect with one another.

At the opposite ends of love, marriage, and friendship, you will see what happens when the wheels fall off the bus: a relationship with a spouse or family member that really goes sour. Some are wiser for it, but for other folks, the fallout from these lost connections makes them want to forget the entire experience.

Does the battle of the sexes rage on? In many ways it does, yet people still manage to offer practical advice to prospective suitors of any generation.

♦ ♦ ♦

TJ, 43, caseworker I regret not giving the "plain-looking" guys a second look while I was in school. I always went for the handsome, athletic types. So where am I today? Married to a good-looking jackass. A handsome man who has no heart, no compassion, and no respect for anyone but himself.

I occasionally visit my family back in my hometown and, once in a while, I run into old classmates—the "plain-looking" guys. And what do I see now? Very intelligent, warm, funny men who are everything I want, but will never have in a husband.

So, you're probably saying to yourself, "Why don't you get rid of your husband and hook up with one of these men you are talking about?"

My answer: because now *I'm* the "plain-looking" one, looking in from the outside.

Rusty, 27, digital artist When I was in college I was dating a woman in my town and carrying on a surreptitious affair in another close-by college town. The out-of-town woman was a true, good soul—intelligent and wise—but she was a bit on the heavy side. I found myself increasingly emotionally and mentally drawn to her, but physically, well, grinning and bearing it.

The woman I was living with was not the brightest bulb, disingenuous at times, with low self-esteem. But, she had been my high school sweetheart and my first love. And, she had a true, mouth-watering, gym-sculpted "hard-body" and a craving for sex.

I was eternally torn between them, until I was finally forced to choose. I knew in my heart who I loved more, but I chose the one more convenient—geographically and physically—and left the other without so much as a goodbye. Needless to say, my only remaining relationship proceeded to crumble and eventually die.

Too many years [had passed] by to look up the other woman, but I did, and found she was married and teaching English at a college in Amsterdam. The girl I had chosen had dropped out of college and was dating a guy who worked in a liquor store, and I had gone on to become an English professor and a freelance travel writer.

That's the last time I think with my groin instead of my heart. I still miss her to this day.

Maria, 24, administrative assistant I am currently seeing/intimate with three men. I am having problems just keeping one man and devote all the time and love for him. I feel so emotionally, physically, and financially exhausted trying to be with each "boyfriend." I regret that I can't make a decision as to whom I should be with because each man possesses a unique quality I'm so drawn to. Basically, I lead three separate lives.

I cannot keep this going any longer. There is no single day that I don't lie to each of them. Where have I been? Who was I with? Where am I going? [These] are questions that bombard me from each of my lovers on a daily basis.

My best friend knows what I'm doing, but doesn't quite understand why I do this. She calls me the female "Casanova."

I deeply regret my indecisiveness and my tendency to "cheat" on my mate. Sometimes, I just wish that I could just disappear from this place and start a new life. I know this may sound insignificant to many, but being in this kind of relationship for almost eight months robs you of time that needs to be spent looking for a better career, and being with your family and friends.

I really wish I could start all over again with the man I truly love.

William, 31, woodcraftsman I was in Florida on vacation with my wife and kids, and was on a bus headed to Disney World. This blonde got on the bus and I was checking her out. My wife noticed! [She] no longer trusts me and the last year and a half has been unbelievable. Of course, during this time she has caught me again and also caught me lying to her.

What the hell is wrong with me?

Susan, 39, teacher I guess that I regret not believing in myself strongly enough; in my youth I tended to listen to others a great deal and myself, not enough. I was sooooo enamored with a young man, only my friends didn't care for him.

Well, twenty years later I still regret that I didn't at least give him a fair chance. I listened to my head, not my heart. I went with the "safe" guy who liked to buy me things. We married and have three great children (don't regret them at all). We are friends in our marriage; I just can't help but feel that something has always been and always will be missing in our marriage: love. Sigh . . .

Elaine, 52, retired I regret that I wasn't smart enough in 1966 to grab hold of my boyfriend and never let go. I regret that I listened to my mother when she told me that all men were just alike. (They aren't!) I regret that it took us thirty-some years to reconnect and get married. I regret that I wasn't harder on my daughter and, maybe now, I wouldn't have to raise my grandchildren. With all regrets, a person should have some things that they are thankful for. These are mine:

I am thankful that I found my old boyfriend, or did he find me? I am thankful that he is just as wonderful a man as he was a boy and that he loves me and that we make each other happier than we ever dreamed we could be.

I'm thankful that we are able to raise my grandchildren; that my husband treats them like the children he never had; and that we can afford to raise them. I'm thankful that my grandchildren are loving children that make every day of my life wonderful, exciting, and fun.

Renee, 34, technical writer I regret not kissing the boy I was totally in love with when we were about fifteen years old. He was my best friend in the whole world and I loved him so much, it hurt. I'm not sure if he knew that or even if he felt the same way.

That summer, we decided to help his mom clean out the garage. It was a big garage and she was a packrat, so this project took a couple of weeks. One day we started goofing off and I started tickling him. He took just so much of that and then grabbed my arms and said, "So, are you gonna kiss me or what?"

Like a total idiot I told him I'd have to think about it. AARRGGHH! Could I have been more stupid? Anyway, that was the first and last chance I ever got.

We've remained very close friends. We're each married now (to other people). He's a minister with five kids; I have a daughter. I don't get to see him very often, but when I do, that old, heart-pounding feeling is still there. Sometimes, I dream about us together and then my husband wonders why I'm such a bitch that day. I don't know if my life would have been better if I had kissed him, but at least I wouldn't have to regret what might have been.

Name withheld, 21, college student I had always looked forward to my first kiss. I wanted it to be something special, shared with someone I loved. However, at seventeen, I was depressed, lonely, and had no friends. (They had all moved away.) The Internet was my "socialization."

One night I met someone online my age that happened to bear my favorite male name. He lived fairly close to me, so he asked if he could call me since there would be no long distance. I said, "Yes . . . I loved having someone to talk to." So, we talked for a little bit and I could tell he was flirting with me. Then he asked me if he could meet me. My heart was pounding; I was slightly afraid. After all, I had heard so many awful stories about these meetings, but my common sense seemed to fail me that night, and I said, "Yes."

I went and told my parents who were rightly upset, and my mother insisted on staying home that morning to meet him. (I won't get into my parents and their feelings, for they aren't to blame. I'll just stick to the story.)

He came over the next morning and when we were alone, he wanted to see my bedroom. I don't know what possessed me to do all of this, but I, of course, showed him my room. For some reason we were sitting on the floor and all of a sudden I saw his head coming down and before I knew it, he was kissing me. And to make a long story short, I regret my stupid action.

I could have been raped, murdered . . . you name it. But my biggest regret was that he had taken that first kiss from me and it wasn't what I had wanted—what I had dreamed of. It wasn't romantic; it was pure lust. I still carry that regret with me and I don't think I'll ever *stop* regretting it.

Name withheld, 45, gardener "My mother taught me right," as they say. I grew up a polite boy and an Eagle Scout. I finally discovered friends and girls late in high school, and went steady all through my senior year; and after graduation, with one girl who was one year younger than me. We weren't a perfect match, but we seemed happy. There were times she showed her "outlaw" tendencies and selfishness, but I guess I was still too insecure to risk "playing the field," so I stayed with her.

Anyway, I got her pregnant toward the end of her senior year. I was putting myself through college and working and also trying for an ROTC scholarship, which required its applicants to be single. I gave all that up (except for working, of course) to "do the right thing" and marry her. My college plans, and later, my professional career, were dismissed out of hand because she had to live close to her parents and large, extended family.

She was abusive and selfish and had absolutely no respect for me, other people (except her blood relatives), or even the law. I stuck it out for twenty years "for the kids' sake," finally waking up in my late thirties when I realized I deserved to be respected and to have an opportunity to be happy.

Why isn't birth control easily available to teenagers? Teens have NO business getting pregnant. They need to grow up themselves, first!

Ben, 24, customer advisor Simply ending a relationship to someone I liked very much. Still don't understand why I made that decision; she is now home in Argentina.

Although I believe twenty-four is too young for any serious regrets, reading other people's regrets has made me realize not to waste opportunities, especially time. My grandma says to me, "Procrastination is the thief of time," which should be everyone's motivation in life.

Galen, 61, interpreter I drifted through college in the '50s, dating a beautiful brunette for years. She was attractive, brilliant (graduated Cum Laude), inherited wealth [and] held my father—one of her professors—in high esteem. My family thought she was something special and we enjoyed being with each other.

When I graduated, I went to a job on the East Coast. A year later, she selected a graduate school nearby so that we were near each other daily. But she was interested in marriage and a family. I wasn't, and opted instead for a position in Southeast Asia. Five months after I left, she sent a nice letter telling of her engagement and soon married another grad who was rather dazed at his good fortune. I suddenly realized that I had forgone a wife, a family, and a stateside career.

In the next twenty years I immersed myself in new cultures, learned a new language, and met fascinating people—villagers and pedicab drivers, generals, princesses, merchants, world travelers, ambassadors, pilots, bargirls, and soldiers of fortune—all of us on the periphery of the larger war in Vietnam. A book was written about one of my bosses and I interpreted for reporters. Over the decades, I interviewed thousands of refugees, met two presidents, and appeared on nationwide TV.

During all this, my college flame and I kept in contact, always interested in the latest in each other's lives. Had we married, I would probably be a teacher somewhere, putting our children through college.

I did marry another wonderful woman when I was well over fifty and have settled down, but it is too late for children.

I was honored over the years when friends named four boys for me. One recent afternoon the realization came that I will never have a son of my own to inherit what I have to pass on. And I wept for the path that I passed by, for that which might have been.

Name withheld, 47, teacher When I was twenty years old I had this huge crush on this man. He was a few years older than I and had lived on a farm near my parents while we were growing up. He had been married and divorced and in the service. He was in college and then going on to medical school.

I was very naive at this age and very insecure. He showed an interest in me, but was kind of shy at times about asking me out. There was a dance in town this one night and I wanted to go with him, but by the time he had gotten the nerve to ask me, I had already gone with someone else! I could kick myself for not waiting it out. That night could have changed my whole life and often, I go back over it thinking that had I been more patient and less insecure I could have maybe had a chance.

I still think about him a lot. We used to tease each other about achieving our goals: I became a special education teacher like I had intended; he finally become an MD. I have been teaching special education now for twenty-one years. He never was allowed his dream of treating people in his own practice because he was killed in a car accident on his way to start his new career. Fate has such strange ways. . . .

Bob, 70, retired I hit the big "70" this year. That's difficult to imagine. They say as you age you can remember events fifty years ago, but not what happened last week. It's true. We grew up in the age of much change. Just imagine no television, washing machines, freezers, refrigerators, etc. We did have three newspapers, seven-day mail delivery and, most importantly, good friendships.

As you look back, you realize the most important things in life are family and friends. Material things are good for the ego, but not lasting.

I was discussing this matter with my wife. She brought up the point that when we were growing up, our parents were loving and caring, but there was no communication in those days. We would never ask about their youth, personal feelings, or anything about their lives. As close as I was to them, I find I knew very little about them.

Friendships are like marriage: they have to be nurtured all the time. People go through good and bad times. My regrets: sometimes not understanding the needs of family and friends.

Connie, 45, education For the last five years, I have been researching my family history and have found a wealth of information thanks to the generosity of family and other genealogists. It is a wonder and a joy to know one's heritage and I enjoy genealogy as a hobby.

My regret is that I didn't start twenty years earlier while my grandparents and great aunts and uncles were still alive.

I am able to find names, dates, and family stories through others, but what an incredible thing it would have been to have actually visited the places and talked to the actual people. About the time I started researching, my only living grandmother was already in the beginning stages of Alzheimer's.

So, how does one deal with a regret? I have made it a mission in my life to encourage others and young people that I work with to talk to their elders while they are still alive, and write down their stories and family histories. Oral tradition in families is so incredible. I will glean all I can and record it for future generations.

Name withheld, 51, wife/mom/nurse My only regret is that I didn't initiate a search for my birth parents while the chances of me finding them were better than they are now. I didn't know I was adopted until I was almost nineteen and for a long time, it didn't matter. Then, when I married and my kids started asking about their grandparents (my adopted parents were deceased), I didn't have anything to share with them. I realize it wouldn't change who I am today, but it would mean a lot to me now, just knowing something about them, no matter how little that would have been. I'd love to do a genealogy search, but have nothing to work with!

Abby, 20, student Every day I pass several students on campus—some faces I recognize, some I don't—and I always wonder about their lives. There are few people in life we get to know beyond their display layer, for reasons of time, prejudice, shyness, etc. But I always wondered what I could've learned from them or them from me, or what we would talk about and gain from speaking or simply smiling at each other.

My deepest regret is that people in America don't seem to have a chance to "know" others, partially because we hold a reserve up against the outside world that has been socially constructed into us to keep our feelings and issues away from everyone, except only those few we do "know." I wish I would've spent my whole life understanding this and being less reserved myself. I regret having missed conversations, personalities, and lessons I could have had if the barriers were not there.

Steve, 48, self-employed That I alienated myself from my parents at an early age. It seemed that overnight they aged and died. Now they are gone and I can never recover all those days I could have shared with them. They were loving and caring people and deserved better. I'm sorry.

Patsy, 57, retired federal employee My grandfather worked his way to America on a ship when he was sixteen. He left his family and country—alone—knowing no one in America, and not knowing the language. He lived with us when I was a child and I regret not asking him about his life, his country, and what it was like to take on that adventure. I also regret not asking him how he felt about the wars and Hitler.

Karen, 21, college student People sometimes think that the young have nothing to regret. They're wrong. I regret not being a stronger person in high school—not having the balls to stand up for myself. I regret having that crush my senior year. I regret not confronting the crush; perhaps, if I had, I wouldn't be so afraid to fall in love.

I regret not spending more of my childhood having wonderful adventures. I regret all the times I didn't push myself hard enough to get good grades in college.

But most of all, I regret not taking the time to really get to know my grandfather. He died when I was twelve. He was in World War II, had been a police officer in Baltimore City, and grew up on a farm. Oh, the stories he could have told me if I'd only taken the time to ask. Guess they're right: you don't know what you have till it's gone.

Oh . . . I also regret never beating him at checkers.

Darren, 32, postal worker My regret is that I got married way too soon. I wasn't at all ready for the trials and tribulations of marrying. What makes this even worse is [that] the woman I married was the one who split up with me the year before.

So now, nearly three years after we separated, I'm having the time of my life. I'm living as if I had never said, "I do."

Lorie, 29, project manager I regret marrying a man I only knew for twenty-nine days when I was twenty-two years old.

We stayed married for six years, but he was not a good person. If I had to do it over again, I would have dated him for a long time and then I would have found out what kind of a person he really was. My advice to people is to take everything slowly. Appreciate the qualities in your mate, but take the time to know the negative side as well. Everybody has a bad side; the question is, can you live with it or not?

Jennifer, 29, advertising When I was twenty-six, I met someone who I had admired for years: a "rock star." He had a reputation for being a real ladies' man, and a lot of people warned me about getting involved with him. But I didn't listen because I thought we had sparks, magic—*something*—and I was sure I would be the woman to [end] his roving ways.

We dated for about eight months and then he flatly dumped me for an exotic dancer. I was devastated. I was so in love with him, but I was merely another conquest for him.

Garth Brooks sings about "The Dance," saying that all the pain of a broken heart is worth it, for those few perfect and beautiful moments you got to share. In principle, I agree with Garth, but in practice, I truly regret ever getting involved with a dog like my ex. And, I regret that I thought I was too smart to listen to wise advice. I believe, now, that people never *really* change!

Kathy, 52, retired When my husband of ten years became involved with another woman, she dared me to throw him out—and I did. I believed it would shake him up enough to get him into marriage counseling. Instead, he moved in with her and they eventually married. I grieved his infidelity and my impulsiveness for years. As fate would have it, though, they bought a house next to a cemetery. He developed lung cancer and died.

Now, the view from her bedroom window is his grave. At least she doesn't have to wonder why he doesn't come home at night.

Name withheld, 43, retail My regrets started when I returned to school in 1995. I wanted to do something with my life and had my goals all set. I was going to make a better life for the wife and myself, so I dove headfirst into college—not bad for a kid that dropped out at the end of his junior year of high school. I studied hard and got good grades for my efforts, having gotten on the National Honor Society list once, and the Dean's List twice in three years.

The problem came without me realizing it. I spent so much time on my studies, I forgot about what was important in my life, right then and there: my family. I neglected my wife without knowing it. She started finding other things to do, spending more time with her friends. When I did make an effort to do something with her, she had already made plans with her friends.

I approached her about not wanting to do anything with me—not knowing that it was my fault—and thought she had found someone else after these twenty-four years. I told her I wasn't sure if I still loved her the way a couple should love each other. I asked why she didn't do things for me anymore; I was washing my own clothes, cooking my own meals, even grocery shopping. All this and school and working full-time. I made a few suggestions as to what would help me out, only to have her do less.

To make a long story short, I left the marriage and the state and moved across country to start a new life. The only thing is, I didn't want that new life, and it took getting that new life to find that out. I returned home to try to rekindle the marriage. It was hard—the hardest thing I have ever had to do. I came very close to meeting my maker in heaven. I even found another "love" after six months of being beaten up emotionally. But things didn't work there either, and I ended that relationship.

It was after that, that my wife changed her mind and made the effort. My regret? Not paying attention to what was important in my life and getting my priorities in the wrong order. It is a long, hard road to mend a broken heart and we have two of them in this relationship, but we are going to make it.

The moral of this story is, never to let the romance go out of the love. You can have your cake and eat it, too. You just have to work at it.

Deanna, 22, costume designer I was twenty and my life could not have been any better. I had two of the most wonderful best friends in the world and a brand new boyfriend.

As my boyfriend and I got closer, he started requiring more and more of my time. I started spending more and more time with him, and less and less time with my friends. After months of them fighting for even an hour of my time, I finally stopped seeing them altogether. They eventually stopped calling and I had all the time in the world to share with my boyfriend.

Then there came a very hard time in my life and I desperately needed a friend to comfort me. Since, of course, I had none at the time, I turned to my old friends, even though I had not so much as called them in six months. They quickly let me know that they had no desire to talk to me, or even listen to what I had to say. The door had been slammed in my face and I was left there with no one but myself.

I learned the hard way that no matter how in love you think you are with someone, always make time for your friends. Not only do they deserve it, but sooner or later, you will need them and they will be gone.

Doris, 75, medical receptionist/transcriptionist I wish I had delayed getting married for a few more years and gone to college on the G.I. Bill. I wasn't ready to settle down and then had three children in three years when I knew absolutely zilch about babies. I thought I had chosen right, but found that marriage was a whole lot different than what I had expected. The babies were a lot of care and I was not ready to appreciate them—especially when I didn't feel well.

My husband's libido exceeded mine by 90 percent, and from loss of sleep with the children and a big, fat abdomen, I lost my illusions about marriage. We had moved in with my widower father and then he decided to sell the house to us. After we bought the house, he continued to live with us until my husband made me ask him to move. To this day, I regret doing this as he shared his home with us, but we didn't want to share ours with him.

Jason, 42, engineer I got married too young. I met the most wonderful woman and married her, at age twenty-two. We were perfect for each other: similar backgrounds, similar interests, similar life goals. What went wrong?

Well, for one thing, I really changed during my twenties. At age twenty-two, I was interested in living for the day: pretty wife, nice car, big stereo. . . . What more is there in life, anyway? At age thirty-two, I was much more focused and responsible: God, art, music, family (children), and my career.

My beautiful wife also changed, and this was very sad. She gradually succumbed to paranoid schizophrenia, and I eventually had to file for divorce in order to rescue my children and myself. Paranoid schizophrenia usually manifests itself in young adults in their twenties, but I think that even if she hadn't fallen ill, we would have grown apart. You just change so much in your twenties!

If I had to do it over, I might have waited until I was older. Perhaps I should have waited until my late twenties or even my early thirties. I say "might" and "perhaps" because I cannot bring myself to regret my beautiful children. Even if it was a rocky road, they are truly wonderful people and my ex will always have my honor, respect, and gratitude. However, my own personal maturity (ability to participate in a relationship) greatly improved as I grew older. I am also more stable (set in my ways), which makes me a better prospect.

Now, at age forty-two, with an eighteen-year-old stepson, I get to see my own lack of maturity from a different vantage point. It is [ironic] that you just cannot tell a young adult how far they have yet to mature. In spite of that, I hope someone might hear my story, honor my experience, and practice more patience than I did.

Kim, 35, homemaker A hundred things go through my mind when I think about regrets, but on closer inspection, these things have helped build my character and taught me valuable lessons. I have only one true regret: that I didn't realize how long "FOREVER" was when I married and had children with a man who is not kind. I will never leave him (I made my bed; now I'll sleep in it), but every day, I think how much sweeter life would be with a partner who isn't short-tempered and moody. I am not even to the middle of our marriage together and it feels like it's been an eternity.

Sharon, 45, certified nurse practitioner What is the biggest regret of my life? As I ponder that question . . . I think it is that

I chose to follow a path I THOUGHT would lead to fulfillment, rather than to continue along one that I KNEW had me well on my way.

I should have pursued a higher vision for myself, studied hard, stayed single, and gone to medical school. Instead, I tried to balance what I thought was "love and life." I became involved with a guy who really was not good for me and I became a bedside nurse. BIG mistakes. There's nothing wrong with being a bedside nurse, but it wasn't right for me. I traded my intellectual curiosity and drive for a career that was only sort of what I really wanted, and a home with a man who believed my purpose, joy, and fulfillment to be however he defined them. I eventually lost track of who I was.

Eventually, there were three lovely children and I gave up the nursing to be home with them. I adore my children; I did that willingly and I will never regret giving life to them. But the man to whom I gave the best years of my life eventually "met the love of his life" and I was history. I've been playing catch-up with my life ever since.

I'm now back in school, pursuing pretty much what I should have in the first place. That's the great part. The not-so-great part is that, at this point in my life, I have so much less time, energy, and freedom to devote to launching a new career. My roles often conflict and I often feel that I don't quite do justice to any of them: mother, nurse practitioner, and student. The result is I often feel that, while I'm finally getting my own life back, I may never truly have the one I wanted. I guess the truth is that my life is what it is and I must strive to joyfully bloom where I have been planted.

In my effort to help spare my two wonderful daughters similar regrets, I try to model and to speak the truth about what love really is. I offer these truths to all girls and to the adults who love them:

Parents—strive to know, to cherish, and to honor the unique individuals your daughters were created to be. Nourish the vision that they have for themselves. Model healthy, interpersonal boundaries for your daughters; self-respect and respect for all people as valuable individuals.

Girls—absolutely honor your own vision for your life above anyone else's. Never honor another person's ridicule of you or your choices. As much as you can, do not impose limits on what you can do with your life; always "go for it." Finish your education before you settle down and absolutely NEVER sacrifice your own identity or purpose for the "love" of some guy.

True love never demands that.

Carol, 56, retired I deeply regret giving into the "expectation" that people who were having sex would be getting married in the near future. Although I married in 1967, the pressure to get married rather than live together was still very strong, especially in the Catholic Church–dominated town where I grew up.

There is no necessary connection between sexual attraction and the person who will make a good husband. Living together until the initial sexual heat has a chance to simmer down is the only sane way to determine whether to get married. If you see that the attraction was only sexual rather than something deeper on which to build a life, GET OUT of the relationship before you do something stupid, like getting married.

A lifetime of marriage to a totally unsuitable husband has left me, at age fifty-six, with philosophies of life that are actually bumper stickers: *A woman needs a man like a fish needs a bicycle* and *Could you please, please tell me why I ever thought I needed a man?*

Intellectually, I know there must be good men out there somewhere. At my point of life, all men look to me like my husband: rotten.

Lynn, 41, writer From the early death of my father to the early death of my marriage, my life has had its share of heartaches. But as tragic as these losses are, I don't regret them. They've helped me grow and live my life more mindfully. What I do regret are the cruelties I've inflicted on others. Most of them have been small—even unintentional—and have slipped by with little notice. However, one of significance still weighs on me, twelve years after the fact.

When I was twenty-eight, I abruptly left the man I was living with and planning to marry. Matthew was sweet, kind, and generous—not my usual type. He supported me during a career transition. Sent me flowers. Made me laugh. Made me think. Brought me into his family. Gave me everything I thought I wanted.

Yet, as I discussed marriage with Matthew, I became enthralled with a coworker at the ad agency where I was newly employed. Daniel was smart, handsome, brooding, and ruthless. And the chemistry between us was dangerous. I became obsessed with him and cared about little else—including the person I discarded along the way.

One day, I simply lied and left. I claimed I needed space. It must have seemed I was possessed by aliens, so sudden and complete was my detachment. As Matthew wept and begged me to stay, I packed my boxes with dry eyes. I moved in with a friend while I looked for my own place. And on my first night there, Daniel was in my bed.

Though the guilt ignited silently, within a few months I realized it had burned a hole in my heart. I never saw the damage I did to Matthew.

Robert, 54, semiretired One of the main regrets in my life is the fact that my wife didn't have an affair at an earlier time in our marriage. We had been married for about fifteen years and then she started her affair. If she had done it ten years or so earlier, then I would have been a free man at a much younger age, and could have enjoyed the wonderful times that I have had in Thailand for a longer period. As it is, at fifty-four, I am now coming to the autumn of my years and that is my regret.

Kathleen, 37, bird breeder I regret that I was not more selective in choosing my first marital partner. If I knew then what

I know now, I would have seen the red flags that indicated the kind of father that he would be to his children.

Hindsight is 20/20. Too many times we allow ourselves to become wrapped up in a person without looking at the picture as a whole. My boys are now fifteen and sixteen. Their father and I have been divorced for thirteen years. I do not hold any ill feelings about our past relationship. However, when I look back, I can now see things differently. This man is the father of my children. When I married him, I was not thinking that this man would be the father of my children. If I had been thinking that [he] would father my children, I would have paid closer attention to his lifelong behavior patterns.

When we are young and looking at a prospective mate, how often do we ask ourselves if that person has good moral character; does this person show signs of responsibility and accountability? Is this person the kind of role model that I would like for my children? Will this person stick around to help raise these children?

I do not regret that I had my children, only that I was not more responsible in selecting the man that would father them. Any man can be a father, but only those precious few can truly be a dad.

Eileen, 40, customer service representative All of my life I have had regrets, only to look back later and see how much I gained from those experiences; how much they have made me the strong and special person that I am today. So while I may regret something at a present time, I typically "forgive" myself later.

I have had a successful career beyond what I ever expected. I have had two unsuccessful marriages that I have learned to deal with by seeing that, while they were ultimately bad choices, they were the right choices for me at the time. I am currently in my third marriage and, at the moment, regretting it. My husband is a wonderful man in many ways, but he has broken a very important promise to me. Not only am I angry with him [and] unable to trust him, I am down on myself for being so stupid in agreeing to marry him. I am afraid that I will soon be three times divorced and I don't like what that says about me.

Maybe we will work it out. But if we don't, I only hope that someday I will look back on this and see it in a positive light for the good things it brought me, and not how I see it now. Life is too short to spend so much time looking backward and wishing for what could have been; there is only the here and now. And, for the fortunate ones, a future to rebuild, start over, and continue in our pursuit of happiness.

I will allow myself a brief time to feel sorry for myself, but then I need to move on. At least my kitties and canines love me, no matter what.

chapter 2

The Ones That Got Away

**For everything you have missed, you have gained something else;
And for everything you gain, you lose something else.**

—Ralph Waldo Emerson

Welcome to the land of missed opportunities. You know the ones: the trip of a lifetime. The surefire investment. The perfect mate. The ideal job. In other words, the "woulda's, shoulda's, and coulda's" of our lives.

The missed chances include everything from travel, education, and assertiveness to careers, money, and freedom. Not surprisingly, money and careers usually go hand in hand.

Generally, no matter how much money people make, it never seems to be enough. People relate how society's focus on wealth has affected their lives and they regret not taking better control of their money. Their woes not only affect them, but also the people they care for most.

As far as careers go, so go the "Dilberts" of the world—the folks who feel they are working too damn hard. Eventually, they realize the brass ring isn't worth grabbing, after all.

Underlying much of this conflict is education—or rather, the lack of it. Throughout this book, you'll see how the lack of a "proper" education becomes the foundation for a series of other regrets down the road—some serious, some not.

I'm always amazed when people refer to a missed opportunity—*especially* their education—and say something like, "But I'll be thirty years old by the time I graduate." The obvious retort is, "And how old will you be if you *don't?*"

I'm also reminded of the many public service campaigns I've worked on over the years, some of which focused on education. Trouble was, these campaigns were all the same: rather preachy and normally featuring a "celebrity" or some other authority figure admonishing kids to "stay in school."

My youngest daughter, Hilary, like many kids her age (she's twelve), has never been real fond of school. Occasionally, she asks if she has to go to college when she's eighteen and I always wonder about giving her "the lecture."

But not anymore. Now, I think I'll just bookmark this section and have her read it someday.

◆ ◆ ◆

Susan, 25, social services As I wade through massive piles of graduate school brochures, I realize that my biggest regret is not applying myself to my studies in college. When I left my small, rural hometown for life at a huge university, I was determined to leave my bookworm reputation behind. I spent my first two years of college doing more socializing than studying—and my grades reflected it.

In just two short years, I went from being a National Merit Finalist and honor student to someone who was nearly flunking out of college. I rationalized my behavior as a "growth experience," and that I was learning social skills necessary to succeed in the business world. I reveled in the fact that, for the first time in my life, I was a part of the "in crowd."

Although I mended my ways during the second half of my college career (due, in part, to serious reprimands from my parents), the damage had been done. My Dean's List honors from my final college years and my outstanding GRE scores cannot offset my abysmal performance during my first two years of college. I will not be able to attend my top choice graduate school. In fact, I will not be able to attend my top five graduate school choices.

The single best piece of advice that I could give to new college freshman is: *Don't skip class!* When I stopped skipping my classes, I was amazed at how much easier it was to prepare for my exams. Last-minute cramming was unnecessary, as

I had already begun to process the information simply by listening to the lecture.

The second piece of advice I would give is to take full advantage of the academic opportunities offered to you. Otherwise, you're wasting your tuition dollars.

Heather, 42, administrative assistant I regret smoking too much marijuana in high school and college—too much partying in general—which led to a lack of direction and a lack of a goal for the future.

I regret a stupid, two-year love affair in high school and college and the stupidity on my part that led to two abortions, although I am thankful for *Roe vs. Wade*. Having a child from that relationship would have been a huge mistake for all involved. I regret that lack of direction in college because I spent the rest of my adult life playing catch-up in the job market.

However, it is proving to be a good lesson for my two daughters, ages sixteen and nineteen, because they have witnessed how hard I have had to work to catch up and, so far, my nineteen-year-old is on track in college and goal-oriented. My sixteen-year-old tends to "ride the shoulder," but I know we have instilled the very basic things she needs to make it as an adult.

I regret having to work long hours when my girls were little, and not having the energy left to spend the kind of time with them I probably should have. I hope that's what grandparenting is all about: time to spend on the little things that slipped through the cracks as my husband and I built a life for our family.

Each day, I regret the time I don't take . . . with friends and family, but am always working toward fostering friendships and family relationships, because those are the really important things in my life. . . .

Jennifer, 33, housewife/struggling writer This is so easy! I have had this regret for twelve years now and, I might add, it is my one and only regret, but is costing me dearly.

When I was in college, I went for the major that would make me the most money instead of focusing on the major that I loved, that was my dream, that made my soul quake, that made me jump for joy.

I chose business administration over writing. I was miserable. I hated calculus and quantitative analysis, economics and marketing. But everyone said, "Graduate with a degree in business and you can land any job."

I was struggling halfway through my second calculus course and only a year from graduating, when I woke up—finally! I decided to follow my heart and pursue a degree in English and writing even if it meant staying another year in college. I got my degree in writing, but had no course of action as what to do with it. Where would I work? So I married instead, moved to Florida, and helped my husband fulfill his lifelong dream of flying fighter jets in the Navy.

About five years ago I decided to start writing, seriously.

But I had lost so much time. I had no connections in the writing field and had to start at the very beginning. I read every book I could get my hands on; I signed up on the Internet; I met other writers and joined writing groups.

It has been a hard, long process, but slowly I have been building a résumé of writing credits and getting my name out in the writing industry. I know, however, had I stayed focused and followed my first love—writing—that my college days would have been much better. I would have focused on writing and gotten involved with the school paper; maybe done an internship or co-op and would have had a better connection with my teachers. I would have been happier and I'm sure my grades would have reflected this.

Sometimes we have to learn the hard way and although this is my one and only regret in life, it is not holding me back from fulfilling my dream of becoming the best writer I can be.

Linda, 43, housecleaner I have many regrets in my life, but the one thing I regret most is not pursuing my dream of becoming a nurse. This is something I have wanted to do since I was in high school. I even put in the yearbook that I would become a nurse. I like to help people and I feel this would be the ultimate way of doing that. I have thought about pursuing this dream, but unfortunately, I talked myself out of going back to school. I never went any further than high school.

I am now forty-three, and will never pursue this dream. I feel I am too old to go to college and it would be too difficult, so I am cleaning other people's homes. If I could do my life over I would go to college and become that nurse I have always wanted to be.

David, 32, contract computer engineer The regret I have is that I allowed the California public school system to control how my life and education would be shaped. I was transferred to a public school from a private school for the seventh grade. I had previously been working at an eighth-grade level in the sixth grade, but when I was transferred to the public school, they put me at an accelerated seventh-grade level without testing me. To say the least, I went crazy.

I decided not to do any homework and do only the least amount to pass the class. As it was mostly old hash to me, I didn't have to do much to pass, and for the seventh and eighth grades, I slid through without problems. But I didn't stop there. I continued to slack off during my freshman and sophomore years in high school. In the sixth grade, few of my teachers could keep up with me; by the ninth grade, no one had to even struggle to keep up with me. I was still intellectually above my fellow peers, but my grades showed something else.

Finally, in my junior year, I decided to take back my life and show what I was truly capable of. Unfortunately, the damage had been done and my GPA was too low to get into any good university, let alone get any scholarships or grants. So I am still working at getting a degree, and past mistakes have caused a lot of hopes to have to be put on hold.

Richard, 24, civil servant I regret not going to university when I had the chance. Instead, I left school three-quarters of the way through my A-levels to work in the Civil Service. My job is the typical government job—working 9 till 5. I sometimes think how different my life could have been if I had gone to university to study drama. I know it's not too late to go now, but it's never the same when you're that bit older. I'm sure you could never enjoy it as much. I mean, let's be honest here: you can always spot the mature students at college!

Lynelle, 29, homemaker I would never change the way my life has turned out, but sometimes I wish I could go back and change the way it came to be.

I wish I had taken school more seriously [and then] I would have been able to accomplish my dream of becoming a veterinarian. Instead, I just goofed off a lot and by the time I was a senior in high school, I was expecting my first child. I loved my boyfriend and we had already made plans to get married, so this just amplified those plans and we got married that December. So here I was, a senior in high school, married, and expecting a baby. I knew I was not going to receive a diploma, but I stuck it out anyway and finished high school.

My daughter was born two weeks before graduation. I missed my prom (because I was eight months pregnant); I missed my grad night party (because I had a new baby); and I missed being able to go back and get my diploma (I was only two credits short) so I could go on to college. So, is my regret having a baby? Getting married? No, my regret is not listening to my own instincts and saying "No" to the first man I ever said "Yes" to.

I have been married for ten years now; we have five great kids and I don't regret any of it. I just wish it had come about under different circumstances. You never will know how much these small things (prom, grad night, etc.) mean to you until you have missed out on them and you can never go back! I will never be able to have those experiences and that is my regret.

Wendy, 46, deli manager My one and true regret is that I did not apply myself in school, in so much as to not fulfill my dream in life. Instead, I followed my friends in what was "cool" and acceptable in life . . . in the late '60s and early '70s.

My parents didn't push; they were content with what I did and [didn't ask for] better—even though I know that I could have done much, much more. I was destined to marry young, just as my mother did, and raise a family. Only after they were in high school and I went back to college, did I realize how much I really missed. If, way back when, I followed my dream, I would not be stuck in a middle-of-the-road job in a grocery store, without a college education, trying at forty-six to eke out a living.

With a better education, I know I could have done better if only I had applied myself. I tried very hard to instill this into my children and I hope that they will succeed much better than I did, and will be better prepared for the life ahead.

Denise, 25, administrative assistant In my limited experience, I have learned that those choices we make that change the course of our lives should not be looked at as regrets, but as a learning experience.

At the age of nineteen, I met the love of my life. We were attending separate colleges, yet that did not stop the romance: we were engaged within two years. At twenty-two, and just three semesters short of graduating, I discovered I was pregnant. I married my sweetheart and moved to be near his college, although I knew that there was no way I would finish my degree there.

I cannot say that I regret not getting my degree, [because] in its place [are] a beautiful three-year-old and six-month-old who bring me more joy than a job ever could. I have never given up on a college degree, I have never quit college; I've just slowed WAY down.

Someday I will graduate, and that graduation will be very special as my children will be there to share it with me. Women often say that they regret not being an at-home mother. I wish I could be home with my children, yet I know that my job helps the family, the daycare helps the kids' socialization skills and teaches them independence, and I truly enjoy my job. My mornings, evenings, and weekends with the kids are special; we do not take the family for granted.

Philip, 52, computer sales consultant Every time I think of your Web site, I think of Frank Sinatra's great song with the words: *I have some regrets, I have had a few, but too few to mention . . .* or so it goes, something like that.

I have lots of little regrets; that one true regret I have was lying and fabricating stories about where I was going to college when I was much younger. I did poorly my first year because, to tell the truth, I was horribly homesick. That mushroomed into not going to class, sleeping the day away, awash in this depression.

After coming back home I made up these little lies so I would not have to face the truth: that I did not have the emotional fortitude to make it in college. I have since gone on to have a good education, although it has been less traditional and revolved around my work in the computer industry. The lying was bad and sometimes during weak periods in my life, I will succumb to those same emotional pressures and not be as assertive with what I really want. I do try to work on this problem . . . and point it out to my family. They, hopefully, do [not] carry this gene.

I have never hurt anyone but myself, and have never lied for personal gain. In fact, it has kept me from really fulfilling certain goals I have, especially for my career. I work hard, have a wonderful marriage, and two bright and very straightforward teenage girls. My regret has turned to a positive for my family because I'm open about the danger of not being straight in everything you do. It makes life much simpler.

Name withheld, 38, truck dispatcher I regret talking my way out of a good paddling in my junior year of high school.

After that, it was downhill all the way and I dropped out the following year.

Kelly, 33, corporate travel agent My biggest regret is not finishing college. I dropped out after my third semester because I was bored. My parents insisted that I go to some kind of trade school. I ended up in travel school, not because of any interest in travel, but because the school was not local (it was in Pittsburgh; I lived in New York).

I have been working in travel for thirteen years now. I have had my share of good trips (cheap ones!), made some wonderful friends, and learned a lot along the way. But every day, when I go to my desk, I realize this is not for me. I have reached the point in my life and career that starting over again would be very hard, if not impossible. Living in New York City, the money I make now is just enough to get by, with a little bit extra for fun. As a single woman, it is not so easy to start over and continue to support [yourself].

One of these days I will return to school—I hope. But with a full-time, high stress job, I keep on putting it off. My advice to ANYONE who is still in school is to stick it out, especially if someone else (parents, spouse, etc.) is willing to pay for it. Leaving is easy; going back is so much harder. Your education is always with you. It is something no one can take away.

The "real world" can wait; now is your time to learn.

Jim, 71, retired woodshop teacher I regret I didn't do more to protect me and my students' hearing from shop and other loud noises through better teaching and action. I realize now I might have saved some of them from serious hearing loss and, in some cases, to be spared the terrible affliction of tinnitus.

I have these ear noises all the time—oftentimes worse than others. I didn't realize the seriousness of this situation at the time or I would have taken measures to protect my students and myself. I should have researched this and known the right course to take. Many people, young and old, are not being made aware and will be afflicted in the future.

Jerry, 69, baker If only I could see the future as well as the past. Do I have regrets? I think everyone in the world would have many.

As I think about the past and regrets, I really feel that I would have had a more productive and more satisfying life, but I still have enjoyed what I did as a profession. There's a lot of blame to go around if my life were to have gone a different course. I could blame teachers, counselors, my parents, or friends.

When I graduated high school, I didn't have a clue of what I wanted to do. I was interested in photography, but it was difficult to make a living at that profession. Meteorology interested me, but I thought how many unemployed meteorologists there must be? Becoming a doctor was out of the question because I could never pass a chemistry course that I knew was required.

Since there was no one to really discuss my dilemma with, I went to UCLA and decided to major in education. I knew that there was a demand for teachers and I always loved school. The only thing that worried me was my dislike for small children. I thought that might change as I got older.

After transferring to Los Angeles City College (LACC)—because [I despised] ROTC which was required at UCLA, but not at LACC—[I passed] by many television stations and [thought] this is what I want to do: I want to be a television cameraman, news cameraman, technician, or whatever. But in the back of my mind I figured that most positions were probably filled by now. After all, this was 1949 and television was already around for four years.

At any rate, my dad wanted to go into the bakery business and if I didn't support and help him get started, he would never have had his dream of not working as an employee anymore. And he was getting old; he was fifty.

After many successful years in the bakery business, I actually found out that I had a tremendous amount of artistic talent. I never realized that I could make beautiful birthday, wedding and special occasion cakes. This artistic ability was recognized by my fourth-grade teacher, but was not made aware to me.

Even though I enjoyed the years . . . working in the bakery profession, I regret that I didn't take a different course. If I had gotten guidance at an earlier age and encouragement for my talents and abilities, I know I would have had a more fulfilling and exciting profession.

When I was young, parents didn't seem as interested or concerned about their children's future as they are today. In many respects, even though they show more interest, I'm not sure it really makes that much of a difference. I mean, do they turn out much better? I really don't know.

[My father wrote this—in longhand—and mailed it to me shortly before his seventieth birthday. Until then, I knew little about his education and even less about how he got into his chosen profession. Of course, I also never thought to ask.]

Mandy, 21, stay-at-home mom I thought about this for a while: about why I married so young, six days after my eighteenth birthday. I thought about the three-year-old daughter that I am trying to raise while trying to raise myself. But those are not my regrets.

My main regret is wishing time away and not enjoying this second. I wished I were sixteen, then eighteen, then twenty-one. Now I am twenty-one and wonder where all the time went. I feel like I missed my childhood trying to grow up.

Ken, 39, share valuer I regret no longer working for the government (eighteen years) and moving to the commercial world. It's easier to spend money than to make money!

Michelle, 30, sales manager My largest regret by any means is my desire to work, and to become the first female sales manager in my field. I neglected my children and my own personal life. I was so obsessed, I saw nothing but Vince Lombardi's quote that there is no place for second; I only knew that first was my only place. I used everyone and did whatever it took to be the #1 manager in my field. I have said my apologies to my family, but how do I ever get back their first steps and all of the little hugs I missed?

Name withheld, 38, journalist I regret dedicating so many hours of my life to my work instead of my family. It seems the more money I made, the more I spent. And it never bought me happiness.

Jim, 32, architecture I regret not taking a summer off—either in high school or college—to live and work at the beach. What I wouldn't give now for the freedom of waking up late, working a brainless job for a couple hours a day, and sitting on the beach until sunset.

Anders, 26, graduate student I regret being an escapist. I'm twenty-six years old, very smart, and still with the option to make a career in corporate business. I regret squandering these past six years studying business and administration—something that makes me choke.

I wish I had taken some of those wrong turns instead of just standing [and] staring down the road with my hands in my pockets and my head in the clouds. I used to regret not following my dreams; now I regret not having any except the one where I'm being strangled. I wish I had not been stoned enough to figure this out.

Jenne, 34, housewife/mother My first regret has only just recently manifested itself. For the past five years I have been running a business. I was forced to give it up five months ago due to circumstances beyond my control. I thought I wanted money; that's what drove me to work up to eighteen hours a day and not complain! Stupid or what?

It wasn't until I gave the business up and began to reflect, that I realized it was a waste of five years. I suddenly realized one day, money was not the reason I kept going. It was just that I was so busy, I never allowed myself time to think about what I really wanted! Still not sure what that is, but I'm working on it. I feel as though I now have control of my life again, and feel a lot better for it.

Yes, we need money to live, but there is so much greed nowadays and I just went along for the ride I guess; just got sucked into the consumer age that we live in. I'm just glad I saw sense before I wasted the rest of my life! I may be broke, but I'm a damn sight happier nowadays.

Biff, 28, dockworker I had the opportunity to work full-time with one of the "big three" automotive companies, but where I currently worked, they said I would soon be promoted. I didn't take the automotive job and I DIDN'T GET PROMOTED. I REGRET NOT TAKING THE AUTOMOTIVE JOB.

Sheryl, 42, homemaker When I was eighteen, my father went with me to a bank to co-sign a small loan. He told me to pay it off before I bought anything else and not to get deeply into debt. Today, with a debt of more than $40,000, I regret not heeding his free advice.

Name withheld, 31, self-employed At the age of twenty-five, I was divorced and the mother of a darling, one-year-old little girl. I was so concerned with proving to the world that I could support myself and my daughter "just fine" that I never took the time to plan financially. By the age of twenty-six I had filed [for] bankruptcy and moved back to my parents' home.

Somewhere in the middle of this, I met a wonderful man, but my pride did not allow me to be upfront about my financial situation. I was hiding so much, that there was never complete honesty. When he found out about my financial situation through the friend of a friend, he wasn't at all bothered by my lack of planning, but rather my inability to trust him and be honest.

All these years after the relationship has ended, I still love him with all that I am. We have remained in contact, but we will never be more than friends. I regret the pride, immaturity, and irresponsibility that welled within me, and cost me the dearest thing any of us experience: love. I had so many people who were more than willing to help and loved me for who I was—not what I could do. I was too proud to see it.

I no longer hide my shortcomings from those who know me well enough to help me, and my daughter is growing up knowing that asking for help is much better than living in fear of what someone will think.

Liza, 34, administrative assistant I regret my year of living on unemployment. I wish I had known—*really* known—that you have to work for a living. Somehow, I thought I could get by, doing not very much and still spend as if I had money. A bankruptcy and credit ruined for the next decade have taught me to stick with a job, even though I don't like it.

Name withheld, 32, software engineer I finished my engineering [degree] in the year 1990, and started my professional career as a hardware engineer in Bombay. Life was not easy there; worked for approximately six months, came back to my native place and under the family pressure, stayed back and built my family house. In the process, lost fifteen months of my career.

January 1992: landed in Bangalore; started as sales executive at a computer firm selling computers. Selling was difficult, due to the presence of the gray market. Due to the pressures, quit the job and planned to start own business. Starting wasn't easy. Met a friend who was rich and powerful; asked for help. He showed me stars and lured me into business of silks. Initially started processing silk fabrics (dyeing and printing); were quite successful. I started seeing lots of money and sticked on to this business.

January 1996: started a trading firm of silk fabrics. In one year, we made profits and were encouraged to go in a bigger way. This backfired, due to slackening market conditions and we started losing heavily. Since I was independently handling trading activities, I was held responsible for the incurring losses. Due to the differences between us, the firm was closed down in July 1999, and I had to take care of myself. It was very hard to swallow, that after spending nearly seven years in the silk industry, I had to quit it.

If you analyse, you shall find so many reasons for me to regret in my life. After seven years I am back into computers, and find it too hard to bear that people much younger than me are my bosses.

Name withheld, 34, male nurse Most young people don't know what they want to be when they "grow up." I was one of those young people. I wanted to help out, work with people, and had a knack for things medical; didn't want to go to medical school because it would take too much time and money. Now that I see what doctors go through, I'm glad I didn't, anyway.

I fell into working as a nurse's aide when I was only twenty, and now I'm wishing it never happened. I'll tell you why: I know I should consider myself lucky. I'm in great health, have a loving family, lots of support. I have to live my life quietly because I am also a homosexual. Life has been good for me, generally, but I see "normal" people seem to have such an easier time of things than me.

I regret that I became a nurse. The stress is terrible and, at times, unbearable. Seeing people die, seeing how families treat each other, being talked down to by everyone; [it] wears and tears on a person. If I had to do it over, I would go into computers and work in a cubicle and not deal with people at all—especially sick, demanding, ignorant people. You may ask, "Why not get into something else?" It's not that easy.

I live alone (not in a relationship) and have to support myself. Otherwise, I would, believe me. After reading what other people have written about their regrets, mine might seem trivial. It's not for me, though. I'm thirty-four, and I am, perhaps, going through a mid-life crisis or something! Just [a reminder] to all of you future patients out there: when a nurse is taking care of you, they're a person, too. Don't treat them like a "thing." We go to school [for] years to get the knowledge we need to care for you. Then we need work experience to hone in on being our best. We work very hard. I daresay, you don't even know hard work until you've been in my white shoes! We are trained not to take things personally, but after years of taking so much, it does affect a person. I'm human.

So there you go; that's my regret. If I could, I'd turn back the hands of time and not be a nurse, especially a male nurse. It's twice as hard for us because patients don't seem to trust us as much.

Kristen, 34, e-commerce developer/owner Late at night, when the house is finally quiet and my son sleeps, I think about the day's happenings and where I'm at now. I smile usually, because though I'm still single at thirty-four (which can be quite lonely), I feel so lucky to have the support … from my family and friends, and for the simple fact that I'm alive. They (whoever "they" are) say that you never truly learn how to live until you almost die. I believe this to be true.

My only regret is not telling those people who touch your life in some way. Whether it be the undying love and devotion of your mother, or the bag boy at the local grocery store who made your day easier by carrying out your bags, is to just say a simple "Thank you" for the things people do for you.

I want to say "Thank you" to all those people now:

I want to thank the doctors and nurses at [Legacy] Emanuel Hospital for taking such good care of me after my stroke when I was thirty-one, which left me paralyzed on my left side. Thank you to all the physical/occupational and recreational therapists who helped me walk again. Thank you to all the other patients in Emanuel's Rehabilitation Program who were a lot worse off than me. You showed me how truly lucky we all are just to be alive. Thank you to all the people who believed in my "silly Web site idea" and clapped their hands for me when I bought my second house, at thirty-four.

Thank you most to my mom, who never ever stopped loving me or believing in the power one person can have over their own life, and with their faith in God that we are never alone in our suffering. Thank you to all the people— great and small—that have made me smile, given of themselves without thought, and [are] happy I'm alive.

I regret not telling you all sooner.

Mark, 31, computer programmer My biggest regret was studying biology in college and then going to medical school. I absolutely hated everything about medical school and dropped out after a year. I guess I was trying to impress my family by being the first doctor in the bunch. I also thought I'd make a lot of money and have high prestige. After I dropped out of medical school, I went back to my first love—computers—but wasn't able to enter the workforce until I was thirty years old. If I had it to do over again, I would have gone into computers from the beginning!

Amanda, 32, retail manager I should have listened to my high school computer science teacher when she encouraged us all to make our career choice toward something to do with computers! It was the early '80s [and] computers had just come onto the market as personal units that could be put on your desktop. No one outside of the industry could have predicted the explosive growth that was to come. We were all bored to death in that class with learning BASIC and COBOL—all except one.

There was one young man who was determined to pursue code. I would like to know where he is today. In case you were wondering, his name was not Bill Gates, but I bet he is a happy and wealthy man now!

Kate, 29, retail management My regret is not pursuing my radio career more aggressively. I was in radio for ten years, part-time. It's not that I wasn't good; I just gave up too easily.

Radio broadcasting is a difficult business, as with anything in the entertainment industry. I had some wonderful opportunities; I just don't think I took advantage of them as best as I could.

I got frustrated. I moved to a new town and chose to pursue a management career, instead. So far, that is going well. But I miss radio like crazy.

Jo, 46, housewife/clerical specialist That I didn't do something about my great love of horses when I was young enough to make it a career. All my life, I have loved horses and wanted to own one, but for various reasons, I have been unable to do so. If I had become an apprentice to a horse trainer when I was just out of high school, or when I quit college after my first semester of my freshman year, I could have learned all the ins and outs of horse riding, showing, breeding, training, equine health, etc.

By now, I could have been an experienced trainer with a waiting list of people wanting to gain a little knowledge from all my vast experience in dealing with horses. I could have owned my own stables, raised a certain breed of horse and had a job I loved and looked forward to each day. Instead, I have had different clerical type jobs all my life and am currently in a job that is mediocre at best—in the public sector—and except for the good people I work with, I really dislike my job and getting up every morning to go and sit in front of a computer and input data for people I don't even know or care to know. What a drag!

I have heard it said that you are never too old to learn something new, but forty-six years old is too old to begin trying to be a horse trainer.

I do, on occasion, "horse-sit" for other people who have realized their dream and own their own horses. I can take care of their horses while they go on vacation, and I can go to horse shows and watch others participate in showing their beautiful horses. At least then, I am around those noble animals once in a while. But oh, to have been wise enough to have begun making my dream come true when I was young and could take on the world. That shall be my greatest regret till I leave this mortal existence!

Karen, 44, housewife That I have not written all the children's books I planned to write. The "books" are everywhere—on scraps of paper, in notebooks and envelopes. I bought my computer four years ago to help with the organization of my writing and I haven't even started!

I never knew I had the knack for writing until I started writing stories for my children to teach them to read. I have even written stories for classes at my kids' schools and they have made special drawings of the stories. I would write stories with the child as the main character. These are my children's favorite stories. Hopefully, the children will help me recall all the stories I wrote when I start putting everything on the computer.

Kathy, 48, administrative assistant My biggest regret in life is moving from my hometown. I accepted a transfer with the company [where] I had worked for seventeen years. How I wish I had never accepted the position. I would still be in my little town, very happy with my little house and a very happy life. Instead, I live in the Portland area and try to make the best of a bad situation.

How I truly wish I could go back and live happily ever after. A do-over would be great for the last eight years. I could go back and be HAPPY!

Joe, 42, executive I am a true fanatic when it comes to football. I played it when I was in high school and have been a New York Giants' fan for as long as I can remember (probably the result of my father's obsession with them). My regret is that I did not stick with the sport through college. I love the sport so much that I miss not having taken it further. Even if I didn't develop into a professional player, being a part of the sport in some capacity (e.g., coach, agent, sports reporter, etc.) would have been just as gratifying.

Brenda, 42, disabled I regret that, in the past, I was given a once-in-a-lifetime career opportunity and I failed to take it because I didn't want to cause waves in my marriage.

I have a natural artistic flair and also a love of jewelry, especially silver and turquoise. I met a man whom I bought a couple of rings from, and we discussed my love of that type of jewelry. He told me that he would teach me the craft of silversmithing along with the art of stone polishing that he had learned from a Native American for $100. He also told me that I could use his tools and equipment until I had established myself to where I could afford to buy my own, and all I needed to do was purchase my own silver.

My regret is that I was working . . . seven days a week, as a cleaner with my now ex-husband, and he felt we did not have enough money for me to do that. The gentleman who made me that offer passed away a few years back (he was only in his mid-forties), but now, I can no longer have that opportunity again. Since I had a virus attack [to] my heart's immune system three years ago, I have been unable to work. If I would have taken that man up on that . . . opportunity, I could be making the kind of jewelry I love—selling it, repairing items that were bought elsewhere, etc. Plus, to make matters worse, there are very few silversmiths around anymore. It has become a dying trade, so I know I would have been very successful had I pursued the dream of my life.

Thomas, 58, optometrist When I was five years old, I begged my mother to let me take guitar lessons. I took lessons for about a year, but eventually begged my mother to let me quit so I could go outside and play with my friends. She did her best to talk me out of it, but I insisted. She finally agreed.

What makes me regret my actions was the fact that my guitar teacher had taught for many years, and she related to my mother that of all the hundreds of students she had had over the years, for my age I was, by far, the most talented and she was extremely disappointed that I had quit.

Even though I eventually became very successful in my life, every once in awhile I think about what may have been if I had not quit my lessons.

Name withheld, 25, law student When I was in my first year of high school, I was two years younger than everyone else in my class. I had skipped two grades when I was little and it made me a prime target for everyone's derision, jealousy, and rage. I lived on a Naval Base with my wonderful family, but going to school was an absolute nightmare. I had only a few friends and some nice teachers, but the bus ride to and from school was the true nightmare.

Every day, as I got on, the "fun" would start until I was finally dropped off with my sister at school or at home. The "fun" would consist of the tenth- and eleventh-graders pounding me on the back of the head, slapping my neck, throwing spitballs at me, yelling at me, threatening me, tripping me, calling me names, kicking me, etc. It started the first day I rode the bus (a neighboring high school boy had told all his friends about the "new girl," so they were ready for me), and continued until my mother finally transferred me out of school. I came home crying many times, and thinking about killing myself to escape from what a twelve-year-old girl thinks of [as] an impossible and never-ending trauma.

Keep in mind the difference between a twelve-year-old GIRL and fifteen- and sixteen-year-old BOYS—the size, the experience, the jadedness—and you'll understand why I was terrified.

To this day, I wonder what would have happened if I [had] stood up to them. Physical abuse was bad enough; could I have told them off without being beaten to a pulp? If I had stood up to them, would my life have been different, somehow, in those years before I learned to gain back control of my self-esteem and my life?

I try my hardest NEVER to regret ANYTHING, as I feel it pulls you back from looking at the future and I believe that it is completely useless, since you can't go back and do it all again—and it certainly doesn't help to relive it. But if there was anything in my life that I regret NOT doing, it would be standing up for myself and saying something or doing something so shaming to them, so humiliating, that they would never touch me or talk to me with anything but respect.

At a time of life when that strength would have come in handy, I lost my opportunity to give that gift of courage to myself and sometimes I do wonder, "What if . . . ?"

Em, 24, legal assistant I wish that I had taken more chances as a child. I was a shy little girl and always felt that I was different than the rest of the kids my age (come to find out, years later, that I am different: I'm a lesbian). I had a few friends, but that was subject to change every new school year.

I thank heavens that my mother pushed me to do several things before I got out of high school! Thanks to her, I went skiing (horribly, but still . . .); I got the opportunity to visit New York City; I went ice-skating and was a member of the concert and marching band (however nerdy that may sound).

To this day, I'm glad I got those few chances, although I fought my mother all the way! Thanks, Mom!

Kristin, 25, parent An honest regret at twenty-five? Yep, I have one. Actually, probably more than just one, but this would be one that sticks out in my mind. I regret that I never saved myself for marriage. I never had any "goals" to do so, either. "Why should I wait?" I'd ask myself. Now I ask, "Why *didn't* I wait?"

I was only sixteen when I lost my virginity. I had been dating the guy for about six months; we were truly "in love." My mom found my birth control pills and took them away. She forbid me to see my boyfriend who, of course, I just kept seeing behind her back.

This is where my path of regrets starts. I've been with a total of twelve men in the past nine years. Luckily, I've always been very safe with my partners. I've never had an STD [sexually transmitted disease], and I didn't get pregnant out of wedlock. But it doesn't make it any easier when I think of how thinly I have spread myself through the years. What have I done to my self-worth? What kind of damage have I already done to possible future relationships? All I truly know is that I regret my choices tremendously.

Gordon, 45, teacher At the age of forty-five, with three beautiful children ages twelve, eleven, and six, my big regret is that I didn't start a family until I was thirty-three. If I could have my time over, I would start a family at eighteen and have ten kids. I suppose I could dump my wife and run off with a sex-mad bimbo in her twenties, but I suspect I would be overwhelmed with regrets! Ain't life a bitch?

Gayle, 38, school counselor I regret not taking advantage of the time my husband and I had before children to travel to Europe. It is something we would both enjoy immensely, but with the responsibilities parenthood brought, we no longer have the time or capacity to leave our children for an extended time. I have no regrets about being a mother, only the unwise use of time prior to it.

Jennifer, 29, student My biggest regret is being so "responsible." I regret using birth control, and when my husband and I couldn't afford birth control (we were really that poor), we abstained from sex. The logic being, "If we can't afford birth control, we sure can't afford a child."

Well, about five years ago, we decided we were ready for a child. We have spent thousands over the years trying to conceive. It took us three years to get pregnant, only to suffer a succession of miscarriages (four in the last two years). Maybe if we wouldn't have been so "responsible" we would be parents.

My only other regret is not finishing college, but it is a regret I am doing something about. My husband and I are both back in college now, but it is a LOT more challenging than it would have been if we had finished it the first time. In the last ten years, we have forgotten so much of the information that came easily to us the first time we were in college (especially in math and chemistry). Also, if we had finished the first time, we would have probably made enough money to be able to afford a family (thus eliminating my first regret).

At the very least, we would have the financial resources to pursue adoption or more advanced reproductive technologies.

Name withheld, 55, journalist I regret not having been a father earlier in life. Why? Because I believe that after my son was born, I became less of an egotist bastard that used to treat people as if they were dirt. Am I perfect now? Not at all. But I sure am a better human being.

Fatherhood knocked on my door rather late in life in the form of this baby that changed radically my way of thinking— and of looking at people in general. I wish I had done it earlier. That's my regret.

Miska, 29, consultant My only regret is the fact that I started smoking. If I could change anything it would be that. Because of smoking, I am not in the best health I could be, and my singing voice has lost 1.5 octaves. And quitting is nearly impossible because it helps to alleviate the stress of my job, which I love.

Ben, 39, postal worker My biggest regret is that I started smoking and now I can't stop. I have tried many times to stop, but I have no willpower. It really makes me hate myself and I know it's going to be the death of me—as in gone, history, no more. And what's really weird about this is that death freaks me out! I am a very average Joe, so I figure almost all smokers would give you the same answer as to what their number one regret is. Signed, Dead Man :^(

Irene, 70, retired music teacher My mother always said, "Life is too short for regret; go ahead and do better," but my biggest regret is that I did not look at Mom after she died. The nurse at the hospital asked me if I wanted to see her, but I said "No" without realizing that I would regret it the rest of my life. Since I had her cremated, I never saw her in the casket, either. It seems strange because I know how she would have looked. I also know she would say, "Don't regret it!"

She was ninety-five and a half and played piano all her life from age eight. She played duets with me and accompanied me when I played flute and violin.

Joan, 75, semiretired notary If I had it to do over again—and there is very little I would care to relive—instead of getting married and having children (as a female was expected to do in those days), I wish I had continued college and ultimately become a lawyer like everyone else in my family. So far, I am the only one in my family who is NOT an attorney and when I see my niece ... operate as an attorney, I am truly envious.

However, [there weren't] loans or many grants or scholarships available in those days, and my family [didn't have] sufficient money. My father did not think a girl needed any further education than I got, and I dropped it there—never realizing, as the modern people do, I might have tried to make it on my own.

I actually was born a generation too soon and my mother taught me independence of both life and thought, and my children have realized what, in my day, was not being "normal."

Jen, 23, mother When I was fifteen, my father died of AIDS. I have told myself, "I'm glad I didn't say goodbye; he wouldn't have remembered me. He wouldn't have been himself [or] looked the same. I couldn't go on the rest of my life remembering him in that way."

But now, as a mother, it is all so different. I wish I had had that last goodbye. I wish I had told him how much I loved him; how much he meant to me. I will always remember him holding out his hand to walk with me across the street, or taking me school shopping in Seattle—all the little things we did together that now, as a woman, seem so much bigger.

João, 35, teacher Mine is not a very original one. Like almost everybody, I never tell people how I really love them until they are dead, and I find myself talking at night to some stupid star in the sky.

Ruthie, 65, retired business manager Phil and I met when we were both ten years old. I moved away when I was twelve, but our paths crossed again when we were fifteen. We dated all through high school and eloped six weeks after graduation. We had five great kids by the time we were twenty-four.

At the ages of twenty-six, we both fell in love with a big, old farmhouse and bought it. We had a good time raising the kids there. They all had horses, goats, chickens, pigs, llamas, donkeys, geese, ducks, dogs, cats, raccoons, cows, and even a pet snake. Then, as always happens, they grew and one by one left for schools or for marriage and once again, we found ourselves alone in our big, old house.

Phil was an over-the-road truck driver and I would often go on trips with him. They were always fun. We also owned a thirty-three-foot Richardson boat and for six years, Phil and I would live on the boat from the first of April to the middle of November. We loved it.

On August 25, 1991—one day after my fifty-seventh birthday—Phil was diagnosed with a carcinoid tumor of the lower abdomen. He had bypass surgery and lived for two pain- and misery-filled years. He was buried three days before my fifty-ninth birthday.

Now, I'm still living in the big, old house that we both loved and regretting that I didn't do what he asked when he would say, "Honey, why don't you leave that for tomorrow and come here and sit with me." Why was it so important to me to do those dishes or dust that furniture, instead of cuddling up to him in front of some dumb war movie or western on the TV?

Today, I would give anything just to lay my head on his chest and feel his heart beating again, even for a minute. I used to tell him, "I'll be there in a minute, Honey, just as soon as I finish this . . . whatever." Oh God, how many minutes have I wasted?

Mike, 61, chemist I was working in Chile and coming to the end of my contract. I got married to a Chilean and my wife had never been out of Chile. I had arranged travel [for us] to the UK at the end of my contract as passengers on a cargo vessel, which would take several weeks to reach the UK, and which would call at a large number of Latin American ports en route.

Then my father died and I decided that we should travel with all reasonable dispatch by air to the UK to be with my mother, although there was no question of being able to be at the funeral. It turned out that our being with my mother wasn't entirely necessary, as she was a very independent person, and I regret that I lost us that chance to see and visit the west coast of Latin America at leisure—a chance that, perhaps, will never be repeated.

Name withheld, 50, attorney When I was about twenty-four years old, I had the opportunity to travel to Japan—first class on Japan Air Lines. I was too young to appreciate the opportunity that I had. I did not stay as long as I could have, I did not keep a journal of my trip, I did not take enough pictures, etc. I recall thinking that I would come back again, one day soon. That was twenty-six years ago! My regret is that I did not savor the moment! Youth is wasted on the young—so true.

Rod, 43, disabled (blind) I regret that I did not look at things longer and try to remember them in my youth. Now those memories are gone forever.

John, 48, computers Two regrets: like you, I used to live in Oregon and I often wish I had not left. But this is much more uncanny: I had the same idea for a "regrets" [Web] site at around the same time you did, but I didn't act on it. Well, at least someone did it and I'm glad it's a Portlander.

chapter 3

It Sure Felt Good at the Time

Can we ever have too much of a good thing?

—Miguel de Cervantes, *Don Quixote de la Mancha,* act I

Hey, it's party time: the time for experimentation. Where the order of the day—and frequently, the night—calls for heavy doses of sex, drugs, and . . . well, more sex. In some cases, it's just wine, women, and song.

Now, people sing a different tune as they look back on those rollicking, carefree days. Some participants have learned—the hard way—that life in the fast lane can put them on a collision course somewhere down the road. Others, however, had the time of their lives. And it's not just

"Generation X" that loves to party; people of all ages like to have a grand time, too.

But for those who overindulged throughout the years, help is on the way. People who willingly acknowledge their reckless lifestyle usually find salvation in the obvious place: on God's doorstep.

For some folks, turning to religion turned their life around noticeably, which proves that God *does* work in strange and mysterious ways. However, when it comes to walking on the wild side, there's no mystery about it:

Sometimes, regretful acts are acts of pure pleasure.

♦ ♦ ♦

Sergio, 61, salesman Everyone probably cringes when they think of one time or other during their lives when it would have been so easy to have done the right thing and instead, we do the wrong thing. Five years ago I bought my first porno film; that was the beginning.

I'm an older man, sixty-one, addicted to sex, online porn, and XXX video—and my insatiable appetite doesn't show any signs of dwindling. I regret that I am unwilling, and therefore, unable to shake this as it consumes me.

Has anyone ever felt regret and yet enjoyed the regretted thing so much, they could not give it up? Well, that's me.

Kelly, 21, drugstore clerk My biggest regret is that I was a follower in my young age: whatever my friends did, I did. When my friend first started having sex, she was thirteen years old and I felt so out of place. They all made fun of me because I was the virgin of the bunch.

One day, she got me hooked up with a guy [and] we started going out right away, and had sex on the second day I knew him. Now, they all looked at me [as if] I was like them. Little did I know how much I would regret my actions when I got older; I eventually got worse than them.

By the time I was seventeen, I had slept with sixteen guys. Some were boyfriends; others were strangers. I just didn't care what people thought of that. All the boys liked me, I thought. Now, I am twenty-one years old and I'm with a guy who treats me very good, but it hurts me that he has had sex with one girl who he thought he loved when he was younger, and I'm so experienced. I wish I could have shared my first experience with him because he means the world to me.

I think this is a good message for young girls and boys because at the young ages, most teens just don't think about the future, but the future is coming and you will care when it gets here, so save your virginity for that special someone who will show up in your life when the timing is right.

Angie, 21, cashier When I was thirteen, I went to a party with a friend of mine. I had half a beer and was a bit uncomfortable with the situation. There was this guy who was nineteen and he said I was cute. I didn't like him.

As the night progressed, things started to happen. My friend and this guy went to the other room and were having sex. This nineteen-year-old guy was trying to get in my pants. You have to understand that I was a virgin, but I had told my friend—and the guy—that I wasn't. Big mistake. He kept trying to get in my pants.

I don't know how it happened, but the next thing I know, my pants are around my ankles and the guy is trying to have sex with me. I wanted to say "No," but I was too confused; I had never been in that situation before.

He started having sex with me. All of a sudden, I had blood on my hands. I had gotten my rag. It was embarrassing, but it stopped what was happening.

It should have never happened. I was only thirteen and he was nineteen.

Michelle, 22, mom I regret having sex as a teenager! I found it gives you more heartache than you can ever imagine! If I could go back, I would have waited till I was more mature.... I would probably still be waiting.

Name withheld, 29, nurse I regret having sex too young. I regret not practicing safe sex and becoming pregnant and having abortions at the ages of fourteen, sixteen, eighteen, and twenty. I regret not realizing that all of these pregnancies stemmed from my lack of self-esteem. It was a difficult adolescence and I have many deep feelings about the mistakes that I made.

However, I have been given a second chance: I turned my life around and seeing my self-worth, graduated from nursing school with a Bachelor's degree. I met the man of my dreams and we are now engaged to be married. My family has stood by me and supported me regardless of my mistakes.

I do regret these horrible things that I did when I was so young. I am blessed to still be able to have children. I thank God for helping me through this and forgiving me for these terrible sins. As much as I hate what I have done, I feel like I have rectified myself and lead a very giving life. This may be why I chose nursing as my profession. I do want to give back; I do want to help. And finally, I do want children of my own, but from a marriage of love and honesty.

There are lessons to be learned here and I would not be the person I am without having experienced such pain. With every regret comes a lesson.

Heidi, 39, manager My biggest regret is that I was so foolish and irresponsible at a time when I should have grown and developed into a mature adult. Results from the foolishness still haunt me today. The "party girl" is now alone, with nothing but memories of that fast life. My faith and strong Christian upbringing only makes things harder.

I now feel I am receiving my "just" reward: between the ages of twenty and twenty-five, I had two abortions because I didn't take safe sex seriously and now, looking at my fortieth birthday, not married and no children. Isn't that ironic?

Name withheld, 38, graduate student You reap what you sow. That is what I tell myself every day now. A life is changed in a moment.

I was thirty-five, attracted to a "friend's" boyfriend, and one night did the unspeakable. As a result, I was infected: herpes. He never told me; he never uttered a word. And yes, we had safe sex. I was not the type to sleep around; I was always very careful. There had only been four other men in my life— the fifth was and now will be the last.

I have met the man of my dreams this past year, the man that I have waited for my entire life. But instead of living my dream, I am walking away because I can't bring myself to tell him. My life has changed; it will never be the same again. All because of one selfish, thoughtless act.

You reap what you sow. That is what I tell myself every day now.

Larissa, 21, exotic dancer I was with this guy for three years and he never treated me right, but for some reason, I thought I loved him. Anyway, being a dancer at a club in L.A. where celebrities frequent on a nightly basis, I had the opportunity to sleep with a member of a well-known band, but passed for fear of losing my "great" boyfriend.

Well, it turns out the same night I gave up getting it on with a celebrity, he [my boyfriend] had an orgy with three slutty girls from his job! Talk about feeling stupid.

Ed, 48, computer analyst Being a "nice guy." I was every girl's friend or big brother—always the shoulder to cry on. Many said I must have been a female in an earlier life because I understood so well. Actually, this was very rewarding. But hey, I am male and always wanted women for more than just their minds!

As I was always surrounded by females, every guy thought I was "getting it" a lot. In fact, I was really little more than just one of the girls. But then, at age thirty, I had a change of heart. After the breakup of a five-year relationship, I was quite bitter and in no shape to be a friend to anyone. My sex life just took off!

Why is it that women want the outlaws? The less respect I gave, the more they wanted me. After three years, much of the bitterness had waned and I began to revert to my more normal self. Just in time, as I met the woman I married and am with, very happily now.

I have no regrets over those promiscuous three years. As I get older, I sometimes think back on the various women. I've always been a faithful husband and always will be, but I have a pack of great memories. The regret is that I could have had at least a decade's worth more of fantastic memories.

Colleen, 43, accounting assistant Ah, regret! Wow, this one is too easy! I live with this every day.

About seven years ago, I left my husband after eighteen years. It had been coming for a while. When we were married, we spent a lot of time partying and "having too much fun." When we first met, I was not into that way of life, having come from a small acreage in the country and a quiet life. But when we got together it was like [the movie] *Sid and Nancy*. We are both alcoholics, and carried on that way for many years. Finally, he got into the AA program after almost killing himself on drugs and booze.

I did not quit for a while after. I remember that I still wanted to have fun, as it were. While this man did everything to have me come back, I did not realize how much he truly loved me. Well, someone else obviously saw the good in this man and now they are married. He was, without a doubt, my best friend, lover, and soul mate. I have now been sober for [almost] seven years.

My regret? That I hurt him so much with my actions and I let him go. Also, that I didn't get sober until it was too late. I miss him terribly and have definitely learned some very valuable (but hard) lessons from this.

Jenny, 25, assistant manager/grocery store When I was younger, I lived in Reno with my sister. We were both caught up in doing drugs and partying. One night, at around three A.M., I was in a casino gambling when I was paged. My friend was calling to tell me that my sister had been in a car accident. I was so scared for her; my sister means more to me than anything.

I rushed home to be with her. Later that morning we went to the emergency room, both of us still high on crank. She was hurt and in a lot of pain. They gave her a prescription for pain pills, but she wanted to go home, so I told her I would go later to get her prescription filled. She spent the rest of the day laying down, and because of the effects of the methamphetamines in her system, [she was] on the phone to every person she knew, telling them about her accident.

I spent the day smoking crank, listening to her talk on the phone, and getting more upset every minute. I was irrational and thinking unclearly. It seemed to me that she didn't need me there; she never even talked to ME. Finally, in the late afternoon, I got so upset that I left. It was three days before I came home again. I left my sister in pain, lying on the bed, unable to even move. I didn't even get her pain prescription filled. I wasn't there to help her. She needed me, and I let her down.

We don't do drugs anymore and both of our lives are much different. She has long since forgiven me. I hope to be able to forgive myself someday.

Name withheld, 22, (no occupation given) My biggest regrets are that I was not closer to my parents as a teenager. Now, we are like best friends, but when I was seventeen to eighteen, we fought all the time.

My first year of college I got involved in the wrong crowd, started smoking pot and drinking heavily, skipping classes, being sexually promiscuous. I dropped out of school to party all the time, moved out of my parents' house to live with my drug-dealing boyfriend. I was on a path of destruction and was so deeply depressed (after my boyfriend left me for his ex-girlfriend, who was a stripper), I wanted to die.

Lucky for me, my parents intervened because they love me so much, and sent me to live with my grandmother for a while. I strongly protested at first, but they had already spent $400 on the airfare, so I figured, why not?

It was the best decision of my life. I got sobered up and I've been drug-free for the last three and a half years. I met a wonderful, loving man who is now my husband; I have a good job and I plan to start college again in the fall. I'm happier than I've ever been, but I wish I had not gotten here the way I did.

Jabe, 39, minister I regret being an idiot when I was younger. I slept with many different women, drank, did some drugs, messed up a few marriages, etc. Then, in 1994, I found God (or he found me).

I felt that he was asking me, "You've tried it your way and failed, why not try it my way?" I did, and I now have more than I ever had: peace, happiness, [and] material possessions. I wish that I had become a Christian earlier.

Dana, 36, (no occupation given) My regret is taking a leave of absence from Christianity at an early age. I knew the principles for right living, but chose to abandon them when I left for college. I decided it was my turn to do things "my way." How foolish and self-destructive, not to mention how it tragically trickles down to others. By indulging my own selfish desires, I hurt many, many people along the way.

Partying uncontrollably, skipping school, [and] quickly becoming pregnant, I quit college and married way too young to someone way too wrong. Our marriage was empty until the day I left him for another man because "I deserved to be happy." (Doesn't our society say so?)

I chose to consider myself a "victim," of course. Through my own weakness and stupidity, I lost my kids in the divorce and they suffered physically and emotionally under the hands of a hateful stepmother who begrudged caring for another woman's children. Their father's military job moved them continually and I actually missed out on watching them grow up.

Bitter and disillusioned, I drowned my pain in faster living—having "fun," you know. I ignored good, loving people who tried to help me. With drunken words, I hurt caring friends. I slept with strange men. I chain-smoked for something to hold onto. I maxed my credit cards buying "the good life," and bought a load of debt that almost pulled me under. I lived as fast as I could, and the farther I ran from the emptiness it brought, the deeper I got lost in it.

When I finally had nothing left, I realized what a horrible wrong turn I'd taken all those years ago; how I'd hurt myself, my dreams, my poor kids, my ex-husband, my family, my friends. All those years I could have been building something, and instead, spent it destroying everything and everyone I was given.

Christianity wasn't something that had caged me in; it was something that had protected me from all that ugliness and pain. It was a revelation and self-reckoning that left me broken and without excuse. My regret is the incredible pain I caused and all the opportunities for good that I selfishly passed by. Shame on me, and thank heaven for a God that forgives!

Miraculously, my life is wonderful now with a sweet, caring man and a beautiful home. But I wouldn't be here if I hadn't changed my ways. Those are fifteen years I will regret forever.

Barbara, 42, clerical worker I regret leaving my husband of seventeen years with three children and debts that he didn't know we had. I regret [not] telling him why I left and why it felt better to sit on a railroad track and wait for the train to come, instead of facing up to my failings. I regret that I haven't been honest with the people whom I now come to call my friends. I don't regret the fact that God has given me a second chance and pulled me off that track and let me live.

Jennifer, 32, receptionist My beliefs have only helped me to find my place in the world. It was when I didn't practice my faith that I didn't know where I belonged and took the wrong paths—that is what I regret.

I also have regrets about how I was raised in regard to religion; everyone saying they had faith and believed in God, but only one person practiced what they preached. How are children to learn what to believe that way?

Because everyone in my family was of a different religion, it affected everyone else whenever someone made a different decision as to what religion to follow. It made it difficult for us as a family to communicate and function, being considerate of everyone else's views.

Karen, (no age or occupation given) I am Muslim. I was brought up Muslim, but neither of my parents is Muslim. One rejected Islam; the other was a Protestant and is now indifferent. It was my extended family and my schooling that brought me up as Muslim, with absolutely no discouragement from my parents.

I would say I don't have any regrets, but I have many fears. I'm young, and I think that's allowed, but it's disturbing. There are things in my life that don't fit Islam as it has been presented to me. I have faith that perhaps there is an alternate explanation. God is full of secrets and it's our job to find out as many as we can.

Regret is an unfortunate term because regret implies (though, not always) a sort of surrender to the fear. It implies that the regretter has acknowledged a limitation in the teaching of God. That leads to problems of faith.

Brian, 57, construction manager My only regret is that, for fifty years, I was a member of a fairly conservative church that considered itself to be "the correct one." Only when I felt that the box they had fitted around its members was too constricting, was I able to step "outside the box."

This, in turn, created conflict between friends and family members that are still unresolved. Strangely, though, I have trouble calling this whole episode a "regret." I could call it stupidity, blindness, naiveté, etc., but I don't really regret the time spent within the church membership. Rather, it has given me a base of understanding spiritual matters that is an advantage, rather than the negativity that the term "regret" could bring to mind.

Julie, 29, banking representative I regret going to Bible College. I should have gone into my original field of interest which was biology, but at that time in my life I was all hyped up about God and church and wanted to be doing something in ministry. When I graduated and got out in the "real" world,

I received [one] rejection letter after the next: "No, sorry! You're a single woman and we want married couples to run our youth programs."

I started to get involved in my local church and thought something might work out there. But alas, the answer again was "No." The senior pastor told my parents I would make a good church secretary! I was appalled; I had spent five years and thousands of dollars for this response. So my biggest regret is that I even attended a Bible College.

Jim, 31, sales Pondering on my own regrets in thirty-one years of life, it is so clear to me what I'd have done differently. Having been raised by two very loving and warm Christian parents, somewhere around the age of seventeen, I took it upon myself to walk down my own street and do things "my way" in creating a lifestyle full of promiscuity, drugs, and alcohol. In addition, there were friends (at least I considered them friends at the time) that I would spend nearly all of my time with, only to later discover that none of them actually cared about my future plans, and encouraging me to become all that I could possibly be.

I could easily and mistakenly look upon these experiences as "character building" episodes, or simply allowing myself the opportunity to take advantage of the so-called freedom given to grow and learn from my many mistakes. Well, I'm now thirty-one and I still live with these mistakes that I've made every day. Not once have I considered these shameful events to have played a key role in shaping myself into the person I am today.

Having the chance to start my life over, I'd follow my parents' advice and accept their love wholeheartedly. I'd spend more time listening to their teachings and much less time exploring my own empty prophesies. God had played an integral part in their lives, and even though I didn't realize it at the time, played an integral part in mine. After having experienced such a wild storm in which I helped to create, it's a miracle that I even survived the wicked turbulence.

Today, I'm alive. I'm happily married. I'm a blessed father. I'm educated. I'm successful at my work and best of all, I'm forgiven. Without His forgiveness, [I'd be] a much less [content] person today with far too many bags to carry and people to infect. Thank you, Lord.

chapter 4

Multiple Choices

E pluribus unum.

(One composed of many.)

—Virgil

Multiple choices simply mean multiple regrets. These folks offer an incredible assortment, where no single regret dominates their story. They cover almost every topic imaginable: from education, sex, love and marriage to drugs, religion, careers, and self-respect.

If I had to lump myself into a particular category, this would be it. I've had my share of regrets, starting in sixth grade when I saw red—red corduroy pants, to be specific. These were not just a pair of slightly red corduroy pants, oh no! These were _fire engine red_ corduroy pants that my mom _insisted_ I wear to school.

I begged and pleaded with her because I knew I'd have to endure the merciless teasing of my classmates. And I was right; they didn't let up. Imagine this chubby, ten-year-old running around the playground wearing baggy, bright red corduroys. All I needed were big shoes and a bulbous nose to qualify as the poster boy for Ringling Brothers.

When I got home, my mom reluctantly took pity on me and I never had to wear those pants again. (I think that experience may explain why, to this day, red is my *least* favorite color.)

Elementary school was also the time I started—and abruptly stopped—my brief love affair with . . . the trumpet.

I love music; always have and still do. But blasting the first few notes to "Off we go into the wild, blue yonder" (on my dad's day off, no less) did *not* sit well with my family. So I gave it up. I had the interest, but not the discipline. Besides, I was eleven; my friends were outside playing sports on warm, sunny days and that's where I wanted to be. To this day I regret not pursuing music.

In junior high, things got more serious and one incident sticks out. It occurred in my eighth-grade history class, where I sat next to Darrell, the school's star athlete. Darrell was tall, handsome, and could run 100 yards faster than anyone. He never paid much attention to me all year. One day, unexpectedly, he looked my way and asked, "Hey, you Jewish? You're a Jew, aren't ya?"

I was paralyzed; I had no idea what prompted his remark. I felt flushed, not knowing what to expect—or how to respond. Should I say "Yes" and risk getting pummeled after class? For what, my religion? Or, should I lie and say "No?" I just sat there, barely saying a word. I vaguely remember answering, "What do *you* think?" I tried ignoring Darrell even while he continued to badger me. Funny thing was, he never mentioned it again—not once. That's why I always regretted not saying "Yes" instead of denying who I was.

High school, surprisingly, was pretty uneventful—at least from a regrets standpoint. In fact, I can't think of a single thing I'd change about those years. I was involved in school activities, had lots of friends, and my grades were always respectable.

Fast forward to college. Instead of taking a break after high school to travel (which I absolutely love), I chose the familiar path: continue with school. Do Not Pass "GO" and Do Not Collect $200 (except for tuition).

What's more, I went to a large university (UCLA), lived at home, and commuted the entire time. I had few friends and never felt that I got the full college experience. In fact, I wanted *out* so badly that I took maximum class credits every quarter, went to summer school, and graduated in three years.

I was twenty, but to me, the real world was the world of business. I wanted to work, make lots of money, and travel as much as possible—which I never did. If I had another chance, I would have gone to a small college away from home and traveled more.

Of course, there have been other regrets along the way: getting so rip-roaring drunk at my bachelor party that I didn't think I'd make it to my wedding the next day. After the party, my friends lugged me into the house, plopped me on the floor, and placed a stainless steel mixing bowl beside my head in case I vomited during the night. (I didn't.)

The next day, I *did* manage to sober up just as the ceremony was getting under way. (Ironically, the wedding photos came out splendidly and my eyes were open in every picture; I tend to blink right before the flash goes off.)

Finally, one of my biggest regrets was buying our first house with a "negative amortized loan" attached to it. (In plain English, it means we could never pay off the mortgage.) But my wife and I were naive and decided we didn't need to consult anyone: not my parents, not her parents, not even a reputable loan officer. We just blithely signed on the dotted line. Four years later, we paid for that mistake when we sold at a loss.

Did I learn anything? Naturally. I trust my instincts now, more than ever. I'm not afraid to take risks and I always, *always*, talk to someone who's smarter than I am before making a major life decision.

From time to time, something—a conversation, a movie, a song, a smell, a picture—reminds me of one of those earlier regrets, and I just look back and smile. Except when it comes to the house. That decision still hurts.

Sylvia, 60, technician *"Regrets, I've had a few, but then again, too few to mention"* is from the song *My Way* that Frank Sinatra sung so beautifully. I have always thought that song was very much like the way I have lived my life: I would say that is not altogether good. I think doing everything "my way" was because I was extremely hardheaded.

From early on, I had a difficult time taking advice from my parents. Since I thought I knew everything, I jumped into a hopeless marriage at an early age and divorced a few years later. I never attended college or got my degree, which is a very big regret to me now. I did not listen to two very wise and loving parents who tried to guide me in the right directions.

Even so, I eventually remarried and had a very good and long marriage, raising three sons to adulthood and only one of them inherited my attitude—and he grew out of it quicker than I did. I regret not saying, "I love you" often enough to my parents. I regret I did not have my mom longer than I did. A Mother's Day never goes by that I do not realize this regret again.

I regret short, curt answers to my children when they were little and I was tired. But I am sure they have forgiven me, just as my parents would if they knew I felt these regrets.

"The record shows, I took the blows, and did it my way." So ends the song and also my regrets. I have many proud and happy times in my life to remember. If I thought of nothing but

my regrets, I would become a miserable old lady. Would I do anything different? You bet, but along with age comes wisdom.

Emma, 25, high school teacher At twenty-five, it seems obscene that I would have regrets, but I do. I regret that it has taken this long for my parents and I to see each other as people and not as strangers. I regret that I wasted so much time resenting them and wallowing in teenage tantrums and angst. Hindsight is a powerful tool and it throws many things into perspective.

Most of all, I regret allowing a sexual assault when I was fourteen years old to shape and affect every relationship I have had with guys for the last ten years. It frustrates me that I have let the stupidity of one male colour the whole bunch. I am determined to move beyond this.

Regret is all very well, but without care, it can become a dead weight around your neck. Have your regrets, but learn from them and move on with your life.

Name withheld, 30, nurse I regret lots of things. I regret not spending time in my youth and teen years with the older people in my life such as grandparents, aunts, and uncles, etc. Now that I am in my thirties and they are all gone, I have things I would like to know that now, I can never ask.

I regret that I held such self-hatred for most of my younger years and that I wasted so much precious time just waiting until the day that I was rich, famous, beautiful, involved—anything but what I was then. I was so stupid.

Basically, I regret the time I lost being selfish and unhappy during what were supposed to be the best years of my life. All I can say is that now I try to live every day to the fullest so that if you asked me twenty years from now what my regrets are, I will reply by stating, "None."

Rick, 43, school district administrator I regret spending so many hours at work and not taking time to stop and celebrate the really important things in life—family, friends, hobbies, etc. I regret not staying in shape after leaving competitive swimming. I regret moving to the [San Fernando] Valley! I regret ever making fun of [my former college roommate] for being such a packrat. Now he's selling all his crap to dopes on eBay and he's actually cashing in!

Carol, 24, stay-at-home mom I regret not staying in school, not putting myself first and foremost, and I regret rushing into marriage and a family so young. I regret not living alone or even owning my own car [or] being my own person. I love my kids and wouldn't change that.

If I could give advice to young women it would be enjoy being single, living your own life, being your own person. Listen to your parents; they are not as crazy as you think. And remember: you never marry just a person, you marry them and their family, so be careful—you might get more than you bargained for.

Kris, 47, customer service I regret having taken the easy path in my life even when I knew that the correct decision involved the difficult course of action. I know this has shaped the person I am today and that my example shaped the children I raised. I regret not having taken more time to talk to the children in my care, especially since they are not MY children, but the children of men who cared more about themselves. I regret not being able to talk to the most important people in my life. I regret not having an interest in education when a good education was available to me and my only contribution was to provide some sweat equity. I regret not having learned from the lessons life has presented me.

Linda, 52, comptroller I have but two regrets after giving it much thought: First, I wish that I would have listened to my parents and gone to college after high school. Instead, I got married to a man I really didn't love, simply because they told me not to. I was a very strong-willed child—too much so!

My second regret is that I waited until I was forty-two until I discovered working out of the country. I had the opportunity to work in a third-world country for two and a half years and loved every minute! The experience was wonderful (life changing) and, of course, the money was good. I always used to read the advertisements for working overseas and ignored them. I wish now that I had started earlier and took advantage of the travel and other opportunities that exist working out of the country.

Mary, 49, designer Living with regrets about what I might have done haunts me still, though I struggle against them. My Buddhist practice teaches that one should live without regrets, but I am far from that level of calm yet.

I regret not taking the time for some people, thinking I was too busy or being afraid of being misunderstood or disliked if I got too close. I regret not taking the opportunity to go to graduate school and really explore the ideas that fired me up once. It takes a lot more to fire me up now.

I regret not telling certain people I loved them. My dad was a person it was hard to say that to and he never said, "I love you" to me, though I am certain he did. I regret the time and psychic energy I have wasted disliking—not honoring—my physical self. How stupid it has been to always believe this healthy life-form that I inhabit is inadequate.

I regret never having learned to make music; I am missing out on something I can only guess about. I regret never having gotten a solid hold on the French language. I regret all the time and youthful energy I put into my work helping people sell wasteful products to an over-consuming public.

I shoulda danced more, made a fool of myself. I coulda learned more and shared it with others; woulda loved more, if I had not been afraid . . . of what?

Bill, 56, sales manager I regret being too self-centered and lazy to cultivate new friends and join in early with school group activities. The result has made me a loner, with some fairly close friends who think I'm funny, but few friends overall. If I could just start all over, I would cultivate more friends.

I regret being on the road so often during the raising of my four beautiful and successful daughters. I have a wife who was great and understanding—no regrets there.

I regret not paying myself first, with a savings plan, in my earlier days. It would have been so darned easy. Seems all my marital woes were always about money. What I didn't know was that a nest egg would have offered the security to remove the stress and prevent the arguments. Other than that, I have been blessed all my life, but it could have been better!

Wendy, 30, data entry clerk If I had it to do all over again I would listen to my father; he isn't as dumb as I thought when I was growing up. He told me to participate in school activities—I didn't.

I hung out with the "skip class" crowd. I never went to a dance or a football game or even on a real date. I wasted a wonderful time in my life by growing up too fast (I was married before I graduated, divorced by twenty-three). I know now that he knew what he was talking about.

I would also have gotten to know my grandparents better. Now that I am a mom, I regret that I didn't know them better. I was too cool and too busy to "bother with them" and that is something I can never get back. Even though my parents live in another state, I am determined for them to know my son.

Ulrich, 35, marketing development manager Most of all, I regret having written a letter to a business associate with an "AIDS to her" hate statement about a coworker. Makes me feel sick. I feel low knowing that I went to this degree of hate because of feeling being treated unjust[ly] from that coworker. It comes up every time I think about "regrets" and I wish I could make peace with it.

Also, I regret: spanking my children, drinking too much, staying up too late, spending money on stupid stuff, procrastinating at work and at home, not being organized, and having a low level of dental hygiene.

Also, I regret: stopping my motorcycle on my way to the overlapping stone at Koh Samui and laying it on the ground; subsequently, having made a handstand and crashing into a nice picture, breaking the glass and scratching it; paying money for insurances that were unnecessary; not studying law (I could have been a successor in my dad's office). Doesn't exactly read like a résumé, and isn't exactly the picture I have of myself and I want others to have, but from the regret point of view, that's very much it.

But as I am stating all of this, I must say that there are *lots* of things that I like, enjoy, and find pleasure in—that I *disregret*. (What's the opposite of regret: Is it like?)

Amy, 29, actress/computer manager I regret that I am twenty-nine and have not been fully living my life. At twenty-nine, I see youth slipping away and I wonder what have I been doing since I was twenty? I have had a half-dozen jobs, lived in several states, but what have I been doing for me? Chasing dreams halfheartedly.

I have strong dreams; I want to act. I moved to New York City to be an actress. Since I have been here, I have only had the time and energy to go on a very few auditions. I regret that I never seem to have the confidence to quit my real job and try to pursue what I love with all my attention and energy focused in that one place.

I regret that I married my long-term boyfriend with the fear that it wouldn't last—and it didn't. After six years of togetherness, we were married one year and I left. I regret I didn't have the courage to say I couldn't marry him.

Finally, I regret ever seeing the words: "You've been approved for a VISA." Credit cards are the source of much suffering.

Name withheld, 32, accountant I regret a few things. I have always been told how beautiful I am. Well, that might get you a lot of things in high school, but not in the real world. I didn't stop to think about that; I thought I could get anything I wanted. I was wrong.

I am way too impulsive. I moved to Atlanta right after I graduated from college. I had no money, no job, and a brand new car (payment). I was desperate, and took the first permanent job I was offered in a bank, even though my degree is in advertising. I had too many credit cards [and] I prided myself on paying the minimum balance. My credit was perfect, of course.

One day I quit my job because I hated it so much. (I would cry all of the time.) Now I have a much better job making almost $20,000 more per year. However, my credit is not perfect anymore because I did not get this job right away, of course. I have been here ten years and I am still not happy.

If only I had been a little more patient, I would be much better off. If only I had not had so many credit cards, I would be much better off. If only I had prepared myself better for the real world, I would be much better off.

Heidi, 29, mortgage processor I regret not paying attention and trying harder in math and science classes in high school. It wasn't that I was a bad student; it was just that my interests were more toward English, French, and music rather than trigonometry and chemistry. Maybe I might have had a different career in computers or education.

I regret that I listened to the skeptics among my family when I said I wanted to pursue a professional singing career. If I could do anything in the world that I wouldn't even ask to be paid to do, I'd be a singer. I find nothing else that brings me greater joy, but it's just for me now. By listening to all those "OK, whatever you say, Heidi" comments for so many years, I find it hard to sing in front of people.

I regret a particular relationship. I can't tell you how many times I wish I could go back to one certain day and change the one thing that brought that person into my life. Nearly every single day I think about "what might have been" if I hadn't met that person. I think of how much money I might have now, the friends I'd still have, the apartment I'd still have, the places I might have gone or seen if I hadn't met this one person.

And, I regret letting the one special person in my life go without putting up a bigger fight. I just let him walk out the door and looking back at it now, I realize that he was my first real love and to this day, I miss him. I haven't seen him for six years and every time the phone rings, I secretly hope it's him calling just to say "Hi" and catch up. I'd give anything to see him again, just to see if what we had was real or if it was just a product of our being young and idealistic.

Charlie, 30, clerical I regret not asking the girl I was sweet on in kindergarten to "be my girlfriend" until recess of the last day of school—more so, because she said, "Yes." (I regret a long string of similar timidities toward the opposite sex through the course of my life though I was, at times, quite bold.) I regret going off to work out of state the summer after falling in love with my high school sweetheart. We never could [have] or should have lasted, but oh, it was such magic as I have never known since.

I regret offending my father when I was sixteen, though the offense was no more than speaking my mind on religion. I wish that I'd known he would cut me off for so many long years—in such critical times—when I needed him so very much. I regret that I was unable to bounce my mom out of the mental illness that eventually led to her death, though I cannot say how such a feat may have been accomplished.

I regret having given up on romantic love and marrying for "stability," though I will never regret my little boy. I regret studying things which led nowhere in work, regardless of my hard-won, excellent marks. I wish, also, I had more time to do now that which I know can win me personal career success. I regret the long, lost years of a hard life lived under highly adverse circumstances. And now, I will leave this alone for a while and go spend time with those I love, so as not to regret this evening as well.

Niki, 49, teacher's aide I regret that I didn't pursue something I felt enough passion for in a profession that is fulfilling and flexible today. A number of factors contributed to my not even knowing enough to pursue a life interest, and I regret that I did not have the inner maturity or the outer direction/support/encouragement.

I also regret the idealism of the late '60s/early '70s that provided a wonderful diversion to the facts of real life and real education and real work. Of course, those times did provide some unique and wonderful memories.

I regret I did not—and still do not—find the courage to risk a great deal and thus I feel life slipping by. I do not want to be one of those senior ladies who sit looking out the window, ruminating on what might have been.

I regret that my soul mate from the summer of '68 did not tell me then why he broke up with me (over the phone!) and told me twenty-five years later, when we both were married.

My heart broke from knowing, finally, that his parents' pressure on him was stronger than he was at eighteen, so he buried his love for me in his studies, only to become a successful doctor, but not a successfully happy person because he still thought of me every day.

I regret not having a closer, smoother relationship with my mom and four brothers. I regret that I carry anger that gets in the way of that. And finally, I regret my current (four years) fear of flying because it affects our family vacations and limits my horizons. I love the train, but the time it takes to get anywhere can be very limiting. I regret the thought of possibly never going back to Europe or to Japan or of never taking my son to Hawaii (which seems to be important to him at age eleven). This regret is interesting because I used to be a flight attendant and taking a plane was like riding a bus to me! So I need to work on this regret!

Jeya, 33, housewife I regret wasting my intelligence and not getting settled in a management career I so much desired. Also, for taking religion lightly and not standing up to people when they exploited me.

Roger, 59, hotel salesman I regret not studying harder in college. I regret marriage to my first wife [and] the wasted years in airline sales (a friend once said it was the only job he'd ever have where he got paid to drink). I regret turning down an appointment to the U.S. Air Force Academy (I was in love). I regret not pursuing an airline pilot career with a vengeance, and I regret taking crap from too many people in my life without punching them in the nose.

Amy, 20, student At the young age of twenty, I regret it taking me this long to love myself; years wasted of how I should look, feel, [and] act to make others happy. I regret not seeing how beautiful I am inside and out.

I regret one-night stands—too many of them. I regret letting others make me feel like crap. I regret not letting anyone in. I regret it all, but I've learned to live with them; they have made me what I am today. I'm proud of myself, what I've done, and what I will do in the future. The regrets have made me able to love a man I intend to spend the rest of my life with.

Regrets aren't something to be ashamed of; they aren't a mistake. Perhaps it's an error in judgment or a necessary evil. Either way, in the end, you just have to live.

Mary Ann, 55, retired I have many regrets as I approach my senior years and look back on my life. I only hope that during my remaining years I can change some of these regrets to accomplishments.

I regret that I did not tell my parents and grandparents more often that I loved and appreciated them now that they are no longer alive. Because of this I try to remember to occasionally thank my mother-in-law for giving me my husband. I regret that I have not cherished my husband more in the past, but I am trying to make up for that now and will continue to do so in the future.

I regret that I did not tell my two kids as they were growing up that I was very proud of them and loved them more than life itself. I only hope it is not too late as I tell them now. I also hope that I have instilled in them a desire to leave this world a better place than they found it.

I regret the many things I have said to other people or done that may have hurt their feelings and I now try to be more understanding and patient with others. I regret that I have not given more of myself to others and I hope to remedy this in the near future by finding a way to give of my time to help someone else.

I regret that I did not obtain more education to enable me to make more money so that I could have given my children more tangible things, and also the knowledge to give them more compassion than my husband and I have been able to when they were growing up.

Bella, 71, psychologist I thought about regrets and came up with a couple for me. I am now seventy-one. I always wanted to be able to do research and to have the training and mentoring which would have provided me this skill. In addition, I wished to be able to play music, read music, and be proficient in an instrument. I tried the piano as a child, but did not have the love or the inherent ability to hear the pitch or rhythm. It would also be nice to be able to paint and draw well.

Michael, 46, disabled retail manager As I look back, I find that I have a LOT of regrets. I regret the fact that my parents never wanted anything to do with me and I found out that they really don't care about anything. I regret that I never went farther in school than I did. I regret that I did not marry the real love of my life, Nancy. Even though, over the years, I found out it would have never worked, I still love her to this day—more than my wife. I don't regret my kids; they are the true loves of my life and always will be.

Name withheld, 30, technical support I regret taking my family and friends for granted. I regret accusing a male acquaintance of taking advantage of me—I should have gotten away from him or made my feelings better known. I regret those little, thoughtless things I have done that stung someone else and barely touched my consciousness. I regret the time I waste when I should and could be doing something, but I appreciate that my regrets make me more thoughtful of others. If you never make a mistake, you never really learn.

Mark, 39, civil service painter You are my confessional, my only source for this since, at present, I'm not going to church which would be my first regret, and that I'm not closer to God as I probably should be.

Second, would be that I wish I could control my sexual urges—I lust after other women; masturbate almost daily. I am trying to control this. My wife does not know about this and I do feel very guilty about it. I wish I could tell her, but am afraid to.

Third regret, that I backed down from most of the assholes in my life.

Fourth, that I didn't go to college.

Fifth, that I didn't stop smoking pot until recently.

Sixth, that I did other drugs when I was a teen.

Seventh, that I wasn't closer to my dad before he died.

Rochelle, 50, project analyst Actually, like most people, I have several regrets. Some big and some small, but all influenced my life.

I lost my mom when she was forty-eight and I was thirty. My biological father died when I was a toddler; my stepdad died when he was sixty-eight and I was forty-eight. Of course, all three sets of grandparents are also deceased. I regret not asking them what their lives were like: What they did, dreamed about, regretted, [and] were proudest of? When I did ask a grandmother about old pictures, I really didn't listen to her replies.

Now, I have surface memories of all of them, but I don't really know anything in depth that I can pass on. Oh sure, I remember some of the stories they told, but not the substance of their lives. I especially regret not really knowing my mother. I moved to the East Coast in 1973 and she died in 1979. I still miss her. I miss all of them.

Second, I married thinking life was going to be wonderful

and perfect. And in my eyes it was, up until the time we separated the first time. We just drifted apart and I didn't even notice. My regret is that I just accepted it and didn't ask for assistance in trying to work things out. I now tell people that if they have problems, they should talk to a counselor or someone who can help them. If you take the step to make such a large commitment you owe it to yourself—if no one else—to be sure you at least tried to find and fix any problems.

Third, not always treating people as I would want to be treated. The cruelty of not calling someone back or lying to them to break up a relationship.

Fourth, hiding my worries and my problems; holding them inside. Everyone thinks I am always happy and nothing bothers me. The few times I let them see me down, they tell me I have to smile because they always see me smiling.

Finally, there are two older ladies I know who would love to have me come by or call more often. I regret hiding and not doing that; always putting it off because I'm starting to be afraid to get involved more in their lives and hurting when they die. Which is the bigger regret or hurt: losing them and regretting not spending time with them, or hurting when they die after I have become more involved in their lives?

AJ, (no age or occupation given) I regret having a petty argument where my father was ill and never apologising to him before he died. I regret not being more outgoing and I *definitely* regret that I didn't get enough sex whilst at university!

Ryan, 27, construction I regret not ever recognizing my talents as a writer earlier in my life. I also regret not going to a funeral for two friends who died of cancer. I was going through cancer myself and could not handle the situation at that time.

Name withheld, 21, administrative assistant Hmm, well, at twenty-one I have so many regrets. It may seem odd for someone of my age to feel that way. Sometimes I even think it is odd. Some regrets are huge and some are simple and tiny, but seem to take up a big hole in my heart.

I regret being mean to my dog when she was a puppy and taking out my anger on her. I regret not being mommy's girl and being the little girl I feel she always wanted. I regret not telling her when the babysitter did things to me that I didn't realize were wrong until I got older. I regret wasting my parents' money when I went to college—or should I say ENROLLED in college—since I was only there half the time.

I regret sleeping with so many guys and making myself believe that I was in control when I was letting myself be taken advantage of. I regret putting off going back to school for so long. I regret the pain and heartache I put my mother through when I was arrested and put in jail for eight days. I regret the bad boys I hung out with and the drugs I put into my body.

I DON'T, however, regret the knowledge I gained through all my experiences in my twenty-one years on this Earth. I just regret how I learned them. I imagine that in my life I will find that there is a lot more I will regret.

Maybe I will regret writing this.

Christina, 33, administrator My regrets are centered around missed educational opportunities and romances gone wrong. I passed on a wonderful college option and now, in my thirties, I'm trying to get that elusive piece of paper. I picked the wrong men, changed my life several times, and started over several times. We all should learn from our experiences and life has taught me not to jump in when the passion is running high because chances are, reality will catch up with you and you'll wonder how you got where you are!

The final regret is that injury and illness prevented me from being a true athlete. The human body is an amazing thing and athletes have my respect. Let regret go . . . it will only eat away at you!

Edy, 49, administrative assistant I wish I had taken some chances instead of always taking the "right" and dependable roads in life. I would have spent more time with my parents, my grandparents, [and] my children, especially now, since they are grown and I want some of that quality time again. I regret putting working and earning a living before the respect and love of my children. I regret not pursuing my dream to be an animal caretaker; to be able to create a sanctuary available to the animals that are less fortunate than my well-loved, well-cared-for pets. I regret making decisions based on need, instead of want and desire. I can only spend the rest of my life trying to make up for lost time.

Keely, 35, sales director I regret that I cared more about being "cool" than applying myself and getting a good education. I regret settling for party buddies instead of forming deep, honest relationships with real friends. I regret not paying more attention to the "nice guys" and always going for the "bad boys."

I regret staying at a job for fourteen years when the last seven of those years I HATED IT!

I regret the damage I've done to my body and my soul over the years through abuse of whatever I could get my hands on.

I regret not visiting my Aunt Hattie Mae, who loved me dearly and always wanted to see me (no matter how out-of-control I was at the time). Now she's gone so I pray that she knows I am sorry.

I regret that my life seems to be passing so quickly and it seems only yesterday that I was seventeen—and unstoppable. I regret the hundreds of hours spent in the sun and the toll it has probably taken on my skin. I regret that I haven't picked up a paintbrush or a piece of clay in fifteen years, when once upon a time art was my passion.

I regret the fact that I didn't listen to those who were older and wiser when I was a teenager. I regret that I haven't taken better care of my body—my spirit's only vehicle in this life. I regret that I don't have many friends.

This may sound like a lot of regrets, but my "I'm grateful for ..." list is four times as long. If you look at it that way, this isn't so bad.

chapter 5

Teens: From Angst to Zilch

The younger generation will come knocking at my door.

—Henrik Ibsen, *The Master Builder,* act I

Ever since this project began, I thought it was necessary—crucial, in fact—to give teenagers their own "space." Their inimitable voices should be separate and distinct from every other participant's, and that's why an entire section is devoted just to them.

Maybe it's because of the horrific events at schools in Kentucky, Colorado, and in Oregon, where I live, that I felt compelled to create an exclusive forum to hear—*really* hear—what they had to say.

Or maybe it's simply because I have two daughters and I sometimes feel guilty for not giving them the attention they deserve. The kind of attention that most kids crave.

When RegretsOnly.com first went online, many teens didn't respond right away. It was only when various newspapers ran feature stories about the Web site that teens began to reply, en masse.

And two things stood out immediately: they took this seriously and, amazingly, they actually read the newspaper. (Thankfully, not *all* their current events are culled from MTV and VH-1.) Plus, they saw me as someone in whom they could confide, rather than as a forty-something geezer who should mind his own business.

Many of their regrets rise above typical teenage antics, which are usually perceived as outrageous acts of rebellion. Their responses are incredibly insightful, unpretentious, and even downright hysterical.

Even so, there's one message that should ring loud and clear: the choices we make, particularly as children, can stay with us forever. Therefore, teens should be taken seriously even though they haven't had the life experiences that we, as adults and parents, have had yet.

Teenagers' problems and concerns—or their hopes and fears—are no less important because of their ages, and it's important to hear their voices.

◆ ◆ ◆

Name withheld, 19, full-time student/Webmaster I'm in a unique position in my family of being the only non-Christian and the only non-heterosexual. If there is anything I regret, it is that. Not in the sense that I am sorry that I am gay, or that I am sorry I am not Christian, but because I know that these facts (which to me, are simple facets of my nature, not truly choices) have isolated me from my family, and will continue to do so for the rest of my life.

When others speak of their boyfriends and girlfriends, I must remain silent. When they speak about their love and loss and receive attentive, caring ears, I can only think that I will never receive that. They will never be happy that their darling girl has a girlfriend, or is in love, or has a wife. And I can never share my happiness with them—unless I'm prepared to be disowned completely. That's the way things are [and] have always been.

As for my religion, how do you tell a family of four missionaries and two preachers that you don't worship their Savior? As Protestants, they're convinced that Catholics don't believe in God; Jehovah's Witnesses are servants of Satan.

And me? I am a Satanist.

Not the "Kill the children, rape the nuns!" type that Hollywood and Bob Larson find so fascinating, but I am a Satanist, nonetheless. It's a pathway I've found enlightening, bettering, fitting of myself—unlike Christianity, unlike Judaism, unlike their beliefs in Jesus.

But when I listen to them tell me about how Native American beliefs are blasphemous and that pow-wows are evil, heathen activities, am I supposed to just pipe up and say, "Well, in MY religion . . . ?"

I'll never be "one of the family" if they find out who I really am. Their love is based on a false image that I've presented to protect myself from the very people who are supposed to protect ME.

I guess that's what I really regret: that the only way to be true to myself is to lose the people I love.

Rebecca, 17, student I had a boyfriend who was very disillusioned about God, Christianity, and religion, in general. I am a highly religious person, and it hurt me that he didn't love God. His main problem was that Christians say one thing and do the opposite.

To make a long story short, I ended up adopting his attitudes and slept with him and even tried drugs—to make him happy. But my real regret is that, instead of standing as an example of an honest Christian, I showed him that I was just like all the others: a hypocrite.

I wish I could go back and show him what I'm really all about.

Sarah, 19, assistant daycare teacher What do I regret at only nineteen? I regret not taking school seriously. I regret playing the popularity game. I regret not letting my voice be heard until it was too late. I regret not going to college yet, and having no motivation to. I regret not letting my feelings show and losing myself into what others feel. I regret a lot, but I do not regret regretting.

Laura, 17, student I regret that I was not more patient. As a high school student, I was unhappy and sullen because I felt that I did not fit into my community. I was right, though, I didn't fit in at all. But even though my classmates and I had little in common, there were a few individuals who were kind and patient with me.

I regret that I was, on occasion, rude, difficult, and mean to my teachers. I regret that I could not see through my own alienation to someone who was reaching out a kind hand. I am grateful that I at least realised this and was able, in some small way, to make amends. But I regret that the English language does not have the words to express my gratitude. I know now that when [people are] important to you, you should always tell them. They might not know what an integral part of your life they have been.

Name withheld, 15, student I don't have many regrets in life so far, but I do have just a couple huge regrets. A big one in my life so far is not being happy with myself. I used to find myself many times in a long, ongoing cycle with my weight. Don't get me wrong; I'm not fat. In fact, I've been told by many people that I'm very skinny or that they wish they had my body. But like many people (especially girls) my age, I saw myself totally differently in the mirror.

It started a couple years ago, probably when I was eleven or twelve. I saw myself as obese and gross and I hated myself for that. I just wished for a miracle; that one day I could wake up with the "perfect body." It got really dangerous because I wanted fast results, and exercising and eating right didn't seem to be helping much. So, like many, I starved myself on a daily basis.

I woke up at just the right time so that I wouldn't have time for breakfast (threw the lunches my mom made for me away in the trash bins at school), and for dinner, I would say that I would eat something after I got back from my dance classes. But I started doing all that all at once and didn't think about how my body would react to it.

I would get horrible cravings for food and sweets and hide food in my room to binge later. I was on this terrible roller coaster from starving myself, then bingeing on all sorts of junk food, then feeling miserable, so I would start starving myself again. All this went on for a while ... over and over again.

Then, one day, I was over at my friend's house, and her older brother's friend was there talking about his recent vacation. I was listening to him talk about everything that he did and how he didn't care that everyone else probably thought he was weird. All I could think about was how cool that was; that it didn't matter to him if he wasn't doing or wearing what he was "supposed" to, and I totally respected him for that.

After that, I—very slowly—started to respect myself more. And after I started respecting myself, I actually started liking myself and liked how I looked. It was, like, all of a sudden

I didn't care if someone else thought I was fat or ugly or not "cool." And it's really great; it really is like a huge weight being lifted off of you.

I'm also happy to say that as I saw myself as more beautiful, I also started seeing myself how I really am—and I've almost completely stopped the anorexic stuff altogether. I still have those times where I'm not fully happy with myself or when I'm really stressed out, but I think that's all part of life and I'm going to have to deal with it.

This year has really been great: I'm much more active in school, more outgoing. I've actually had a couple boyfriends, made a lot of new friends, and just been happier than I've ever been with myself. So, basically, my main regret is that I wasted so much of my life worrying about what other people thought about me and how much I weighed, when really, I had no reason to worry about it. I could have been out doing something really fun or tried something new, or making new friends. But I refuse to spend any more time regretting the past when I could be out right now enjoying myself.

Shonda, 18, student I regret the fact that I let myself gain back all twenty pounds I had lost, by drinking beer and eating late at night. I regret giving up all of my morals and personal beliefs in order to party and go crazy with my friends. I regret giving up my own identity to take on the identity I had promised myself I'd never become.

Benjamin, 13, junior high student Just the other day I began taking Torah classes with my cousin and aunt. I have not yet been [a] Bar Mitzvah, but I hope to be soon. The next day, I decided to change my reputation from the nine-year pianist (and by the way, EVERYONE pronounces that "penis" and that really, really sucks!) to the Jewish boy or the Jewish piano player.

So, I wore my Yarmulke to school. BAD IDEA! Also, whenever I accidentally dropped the thing, I had to kiss it and everyone said something like, "Do you know where the ground has been?" or something like that.

Many of my female friends thought of it as a cute little silk thingy that just sticks to the back of your head. But the guys were "just jealous"—or so I've heard. The next day, guys were saying, "Hey, Ben, where's your F-sized bra cup?" or "Hey, Ben, did you forget your underwear?" Luckily, none of the "sevies" (seventh-graders) said anything or I'd have had to permanently do something bad.

In conclusion, that was and is the last and only time I will ever wear it to school. From now on, I will only wear it during Shabbat, other Jewish holidays, and Torah classes. I really regret wearing my Yarmulke to school!

Mel, 15, student I regret not doing better at school, not being respectful toward my parents, not being nicer to the "geeks" at school, not giving more, not going out with guys at a younger age, not being nice to my exes, and not doing the right thing more often.

Julia, 17, student I guess I would say that I regret the year I spent in a hopeless depression. I lived my life feeling out of control and suicidal. I blamed people and circumstances for the way I was feeling, instead of trying to do something about it. I kept telling myself that all I wanted was to be happy. Finally, I woke up and realized that I had the power to make myself happy.

I had always thought that if I only looked a certain way or if I achieved this accomplishment, then I would be happy. Now, I know that all I need is to love and respect myself to be happy. I regret that I missed out on the beauty and joy in life because I was stuck wallowing in my own self-pity.

I know this must seem pretty corny. God knows, that four months ago, if I had read something like this, I would have laughed at the naiveté of what I just said. But now I know better.

Michelle, 19, data conversion operator I got a big, ugly tattoo right after I turned eighteen. It looks like I colored a bunch of bright stars with a purple background on my upper arm. Anytime someone notices it, they say something like, "Hmmmmm, that's . . . colorful."

Kelly, 16, student I regret not going out with a guy because everyone kept on saying that he was a dork. He was really genuine and smart, but I allowed the peer pressure to influence me. Now, all I can think about is how wrong I was and how much I want to go out with him.

Andrew, 14, high school student Right now, I'm kinda happy. I am young, so I don't have very many regrets yet, but I know they will come. First of all, I regret not flirting with girls at my old school. I didn't get the skills I wanted, although the girls at my current school probably wouldn't be able to tell you that. I really regret not letting my life be open to the real world. I have never really had a problem with weird or different people, and once I got out here, it's just great. I regret not doing the extra credit on the math test I had last year that broke my 4.0 GPA. Well, actually, I regret that twice, for both times. I regret not learning street slang when I was little; now, I'm kinda behind the times. Those are my regrets. I'm sure I'll have more tomorrow.

J, 17, student I regret not getting a better start in high school. I WILL get my diploma [sic], but it didn't have to be this hard.

Kim, 15, student As stupid as this may sound to those of you who already completed high school, I regret thinking that high school was going to be like it is on TV or in the movies. I got the completely wrong idea of what to expect. In some strange way, my friends and I thought that it was going to be like [the TV program] *Saved by the Bell* or something. We were sooo wrong!

Natasha, 17, A-level student I lived in Madrid from the ages of nine to fourteen and loved it. The biggest regret I have is not [making] the most of this opportunity. The amount that I took for granted is incredible. I regret not having listened or learn[ed] in any of my Spanish grammar lessons, and not having grasped the opportunity to speak to as many Spaniards as possible. Living in Oxford makes it difficult, but not impossible, to speak to Spanish people. If I had only been aware of the possibilities, my Spanish A-level grammar lessons would be less annoying. Another regret is not taking more photos and not listening to enough music. If I did both these things more often, I believe the quality of my life would improve.

Karina, 17, high school senior/aspiring doctor Most of my regrets seem trifle (as I am still young with a whole life to live), but there are a couple that consume me now. I wish I could dissolve the tension between my father and me. Most people don't notice—not even my twin brother—but it's there. We never yell at each other, so maybe that's why no one sees it.

Dad is in this stage where he criticizes everything. I don't think he realizes what he's doing, but it hurts when you feel like you can't do anything right in his eyes. I pull the straight A's, I'm involved in every activity imaginable, and I try to be his perfect daughter, and it still doesn't do anything. I'm at a time in my life where I need his support in college decisions and scholarship searching. I don't need him threatening to not give me any money for college because I didn't know he was talking to me, so he thought I was ignoring him.

It's so hard to talk to him. We used to be close.

I guess that's what I regret about it. I feel that somewhere I did something to set this off, yet I know I didn't, [and] that maybe something I did differently could have changed all this. Sometimes, I sit in my room and wonder if I'm imagining all this. I'm closing myself off from him because I'm tired of him taking everything I say and do the wrong way. I would rather stay in my room hours on end than be in the living room when he comes home. It's to protect myself from more stinging comments. Again, I regret losing the ability to confide in my father and I don't know if I'll ever be close to him again. I hope so, I really do.

My other regret, although it seems small and trivial, is that I didn't play on the basketball team my junior year. How many times in our lives are we young and in high school? I'm playing this year because it's probably the last time I'll be able to play on a varsity team in my life. I want to experience life to the fullest.

Name withheld, 14, student OK, this may sound strange, but I regret thinking of a theory for a cure for AIDS and not doing anything about it. It's not that I have that much free time or anything; it just came to me and I wrote it down. That was when I was in fifth grade, I think. Now, I'm in eighth grade, and the people who are experimenting with AIDS are using my theory! AAAAAAAHHHHHHHH! Why do I always put things off?

Kim, 19, student I'm still a young kid and all my life I've grown up hearing so many people talk about "If I had only done this" or "If I had only done that," and every time I heard people talking about it, they always seemed really sad. So, when I was little, I thought I would live my life to never have any regrets—they just cause too much pain. Little did I know that there was no way to control it!

I met the most amazing and attractive man in my whole life about a month and a half before I went to college. The night before I left, he wrote me a letter very strongly hinting that he would have liked to be more than friends. I could have the most intelligent conversations with him, about anything and everything. I thought he was handsome and he thought I was beautiful! And when I got his letter, I did the stupidest thing of my whole life: I wrote if off as silly, teenage puppy love and something my parents DEFINITELY would not go for.

After all, the guy had earrings and spiky hair. It didn't matter that he was intelligent, responsible, and ambitious; I just didn't want to upset my parents. So, I read his letter, told him I thought he was a great person, and never let him know that I, too, wanted [to be] more than friends. I just let it go and now, it's a year later.

We still talk, but it's awkward and superficial. And hardly a day goes by where I don't reread his letter, and wish I had written back and told him everything I loved about him. Young people CAN understand real love. Every time I see him we smile through it, but we both wonder what might have been.

I'm stuck with that for the rest of my life. I'm not a depressed person; I'm a happy girl with lots ahead of me, but this is the one thing I can't shake. I had the power and I didn't use it.

Sometimes, I think the only thing that keeps me from crying is the hope that if he and I were meant to be, then one day it will happen. I just can't shake the fact that I could have been the one to make it happen.

Maybe, one day, a more amazing guy will come along. Maybe one won't. Maybe he and I will get together. Maybe we won't. Whatever happens, keep in mind that one regret can cause way too many maybes.

Tiffany, 17, student I didn't kiss him; I let him slip away. Someone once said, "A woman never forgets the man she could have had; a man, the woman he never could." I never realized how true that is. Never let anything slip away. God, he could have been the one for me; I think about him all the time.

"Work like you don't need the money, love like you've never been hurt, and dance like nobody's looking."

Chris, 19, student I regret being so lazy sometimes. I regret being so shy sometimes. I regret not making the first move when I meet someone I'm attracted to. I regret not getting out on the dance floor the first night I came to that club. I regret getting my priorities mixed up. I regret being so stubborn. I regret helping to destroy a seemingly perfect relationship—he didn't deserve all the crap I put him through. I regret not

P.O. Box 42 • Lake Oswego, OR 97034
barrycadish@regretsonly.com • (503) 636-3969

Ka & Ron —

Thanks for having me as a
guest a few weeks ago.
I had a DAMN good time
and I look forward to chatting
with you again.

Regards,
Barry Cadish
The "DAMN" author.

having a closer bond with my family. I regret not learning sooner that I don't have to live my life for other people.

My main regret is not living every day of my life to its fullest potential. It's not a big regret at present; I still have so much time ahead of me. However, my biggest fear is that I'll wake up one day when I'm fifty and say, "Wait a minute! Go back! There's still so much I wanted to do . . ." Life would have just passed me by and all I could say would be, "Damn, I missed it."

And what scares me even more is that I can already feel that regret creeping up behind me. Maybe I'm just being paranoid. After all, I am only nineteen. But that paranoia—that fear—is what keeps me in check; it keeps me motivated.

When I wake up fifty years old and somebody asks me, "What have you done with your life?" I want to be able to tell them an amazing story full of happiness, sadness, excitement, pain, love, humor, and yes, even regret.

Marlin, 16, student Regrets don't work. You only get one chance and you can either regret a lot of things and focus on that, or you can try and make the most of everything. So why have regrets?

Ren, 17, photographer/graphic designer/student I often say things along the lines of, "I wish life had a rewind button." I am part of the first generation of people who have spent a lot of their lives in a virtual world where you can "save" and "reload" at will. There are no regrets in the computer world. Because of that, some of my peers sometimes feel short-changed in real life, where opportunities to go back and rewrite moments of our lives are few and far between.

That's why this project interests me. I have a lot of regrets in life, but I realize that some things may be meant to be. There are a lot of disappointments in life that need to be experienced. Still, I regret not traveling to see my dying grandfather. I was all set to accompany my father to grandpa's bedside, but we were talked out of the trip when we learned that he was doing better. He died the next week.

Katy, 18, waitress/student When I was fourteen years old, I fell in love. Or so I thought I did. He was everything—sweet, kind, three years older—the things I wanted in a boyfriend. Even though, looking back, I was too young to know enough to really be in love.

Well, he and I started dating. I was happy; finally, someone noticed me. Someone cool, too! And then, he started pressuring me to do stuff: sex and drugs and stealing.

My parents had raised me well; I knew that I should not do drugs or steal—and wait to have sex. But I wanted—NEEDED—to please him so much, that I forgot what I wanted. So I did drugs, had sex, stole from people I knew: my neighbor, friends, my own parents. Then I sold everything for drugs and I got addicted.

When I was fifteen, he overdosed on crack cocaine. He died two weeks after my birthday and three weeks after he had died, I found out I was pregnant. I remember my mom finding out; that look on her face, the hurt look. I also remember not caring. My parents, being the wonderful people that they are, put me in a rehab center. And slowly, I realized that I had forgotten the only people that really did love me: my family, my friends.

Anne, my daughter, was born on January 16, 1997. I stayed clean for two months, went back, got clean again, [and] went back to school. Anne has a slight learning disability because of the drugs I used while pregnant.

I regret having to prove myself to people that didn't deserve me. I regret wasting years of my life on drugs. I regret hurting my family, hurting myself, and hurting my daughter. I'm trying to make up for what I did then, by spreading the story that drugs ruin everything. They make it hard to wake up in the morning, look yourself in the mirror, and be proud. Drugs take away your happiness. I regret not knowing that before; I'm still healing, still fighting the urge.

Today, I have been clean for a year—a good year. I don't regret the last year.

Kris, 19, mechanic I regret wasting away the last two years of my life on drugs. I would be high and walk down the street seeing people exactly like me and call them wastes, not able to realize that I was one of them. When I got a DUI, you would think that I would stand back and take a look at my life. Unfortunately, I just dropped further in the hole, trying harder

and harder drugs. I really regret all the people that I intro-
duced to that lifestyle because now that I'm done with it, I see
how it destroys your life and how I've destroyed many of my
good friends' lives. I wish I could just go back and do the
whole fucking thing over again.

Lindsay, 17, student I regret, more than anything, being such
a problem teenager. I realize this now, two weeks after being
arrested for stealing from my employer.

I would "pass things through" the checkout line, not
charging some "friends" for over $600 worth of merchandise.
I got nothing out of it, except for getting high a few times
after work. I realize this now, completely broke.

[Of] all the times I said I would save money, I bought
drugs, instead. I realize this now, six months after faking my failing report card so my parents would not give me a drug test.

I realize this now. I learned the hard way. I wish I had listened.

Name withheld, 19, student Dating a guy that was obviously
gay and getting engaged to him. Luckily, I found out BEFORE
the said wedding date (and before invitations were sent, thank
God!). Now, I am happy with my new boyfriend of one year.

My advice to women everywhere: if you think he is gay,
he probably is; if you smell weird cologne on him, RUN!

Stephy, 18, sales associate I once "made out" with my
boyfriend's brother. Not a good decision.

Claire, 19, student Although I have many regrets in life, the one thing I regret the most is losing my virginity to a guy that didn't care about me at all. I met him at a party and four days later, had sex with him. He acted like he liked me a lot and I was too naive to see through him. He treated me like shit, and still, I stayed with him. Every day I think about how I could have waited until I found a guy that really, truly cared about me and lost it to him. I wish I could have my virginity back.

John, 17, student It all started when I got off of work that cold November night. I was walking home and I saw two female friends of mine at the local liquor store. They invited me to go drink with them. A few hours later I had sex with one of them and got herpes. It sucked.

Sarah, 17, student I'm almost sure my regret will be laughed at. Physical intimacy has become so devalued in our society—and innocence is a joke. Somehow, I always felt that my virginity would hold great value in my future husband's eyes.

I decided at quite a young age that I wanted to save my first time for my wedding night. I pictured my purity as a gift to give and I wanted to be wrapped up with a nice bow, never torn at the edges or undone a little bit. It wasn't just my religious beliefs that gave me such conviction; I was a hopeless romantic and I dreamt of how wonderful it would be to really deserve to wear white on my wedding day.

I guess you could say that by the time I was in my first

serious relationship at fifteen, my pretty "wrapping paper" had been removed. I was still a virgin, but I had given away every other kind of innocence I possessed. I beat myself up for my mistakes for a long time. I made myself hate my ex-boyfriend. I didn't feel like what I had done was terribly wrong, but I knew that I had foolishly given away a precious piece of my heart that I had meant to save for only one man.

I've learned that God gives us regrets and guilt, not to punish us, but to teach us. I found that even when I couldn't forgive myself, God easily poured out His mercy and love on me. He did not condemn me for my past, but blessed me instead, because he reminded me of my self-worth. I've realized that if I am going to "save myself" for marriage, it has to be because of my respect for myself; because I cherish the gift that I will be. Sure, there are still regrets, but I wouldn't be the same person without them!

Bambi, 17, waitress I have very few regrets in my life. The only one I have is a big one: at age fourteen, I dated an older guy. He was nineteen. He was very persuasive and I had sex with him. Now I have a three-year-old daughter named Alana, and I am only seventeen. I had to quit school and get a job to support my baby and in my town, the only job I was qualified for was waitressing. My jackass boyfriend dumped me the minute he found out I was pregnant. Luckily, my mom let me stay with her and I sleep in the basement with Alana.

Samantha, 16, student I regret thinking that any teenage male is capable of balancing sex and love.

Name withheld, 19, college student I was a low-down ho! I slept with eight, I think, people. See, I met some guy when I was thirteen and thought I was "cool" to have sex with him. Then, of course, he broke up with me "because I was easy." Why do guys do that? They had sex, too!

Then I slept with another guy when I got drunk at a friend's house in eighth grade. Then some guy and I started making out a few months later—yadda, yadda, yadda, sex. Then I started going out with a baseball and football hero at my high school. I was a freshman and he was a senior so, of course, I thought it was cool to have sex, so I did. Then I met a dude and dated him for two years. So I had sex with him A LOT! He should've gone to jail for that.

Then when we broke up, I had sex at a party at the university in my state with some dude who was friends with mine; then at Spring Break my senior year of high school with some guy from Georgia, right outside on the beach. I don't ever recommend doing that, either. I mean, sex on the beach—or with a stranger, for that matter. It's not the most comfortable thing in the world, especially after. Then after graduation I started dating this other guy and, oops, had sex with him, too.

You know what? No one knows about this in my group of friends, either. They think I've only slept with one person, two max, depending on who you talk to. I would NEVER tell anyone about all that, not even my future husband. I'm all OK down there, so I don't see the reason. I've never even told anyone that—ever—so you should feel privileged. But I have since seen the error of my nasty ways.

See, I LOVE SEX! Sex is good, it feels good, and it's fun when done over and over. You can make a night of it. Don't have anywhere to go? Don't have any money to go out? Bad weather? That's OK! Have sex. But now, the guys I date, nope, nope, nope. No sex for them. I don't even think so. I don't even kiss on the first date anymore for fear that I may eventually have sex with them or at least do "other stuff." They have to wait. I force myself to wait at least ten months into a relationship. I figure none will last that long, so I never get to the sex and that will keep the number stagnant.

But I do regret being such a closet ho. A ho period. Gross! What was I thinking? I need to thank my lucky stars everything is OK down there.

Oh! I also regret letting the pedophile take pictures of me in a provocative manner and of him and I having sex. Now if I ever become known in this world he has them. And my new man is entering the NBA draft and if he finds out I'm his woman he could say, "Oh, well, look what I have." But then, he was twenty-one when they were taken and I was fifteen, so maybe he would fear legal reprocutions [sic] for having pictures of a minor, or at least taking them and won't do it. He's crack-head enough, though.

Wow! Thanks for letting me get this off my chest.

Liz, 18, college student/waitress My only regret is not having any wild or crazy thing to regret!

chapter 6

Critical Moments

**Once a decision was made,
I did not worry about it afterward.**

—Harry S. Truman

Look up the word "critical" in *Webster's New Collegiate
Dictionary,* and you will see many definitions. One of them
reads: "of, relating to, or being a turning point or specially important juncture."

That's the best way to describe the intense, passionate,
and affecting responses found in this section—primarily from
men. Here, life's "critical moments" encompass childhood and
adolescence; the battle cries of war; and the passage of
time—behind bars. It's when decisions made along the way
can bring "critical" consequences that linger a lifetime.

For starters, there are critical moments in a child's life. It's the time when adults make major life decisions without taking their kids into consideration—and they live to regret it. Some people didn't speak up when they should have or they didn't back down when they needed to. In many cases, the kids are okay; it's the parents who suffer.

The scene then shifts to various times and places, with folks admitting to their mean, nasty, or cruel behavior toward another. What's interesting is that the victim, in many cases, has forgotten the incident. But the "victimizer" continues to be haunted by his/her actions, years afterward. For many people, their previous conduct still weighs heavily on them.

Dealing with heavy issues also affects the men and women of the armed forces. I was curious if they had any regrets about their military service in general, or about specific wars in which they fought: WWII, Korea, Vietnam, and the Gulf War. Never having served in the military myself (I had just turned eighteen a year before the Vietnam War ended), I also wanted to see how regrets change from war to war and from one generation to the next.

To get their responses, I posted my question to several Internet newsgroups, but frankly, I was disappointed by the amount of replies I eventually gathered. I don't know if my question reopened figurative wounds that were best left alone, but it's obvious that some battle scars never heal.

Finally, you will discover some of the most intriguing and insightful submissions of the bunch—mainly from current or former inmates and from the women who loved them. It's a facet of society that most of us never see, and stems from my own interest in crime novels and prison movies.

Most surprising are the regrets themselves: what an inmate regrets usually goes way beyond his crimes and often shows how he ended up behind bars in the first place. But no matter where some men and women end up or how they got there, the journey can often be traced to their formative years—the most critical moments of all.

♦ ♦ ♦

Dianna, 51, housewife I have quite a few regrets: things like not going to college, picking the wrong men, running away from the right men, never having the courage or self-esteem to succeed. All the normal, human things that, sometime in our lives, we think about.

But the two things I regret most are not talking to my children about the dangers of drugs and alcohol and not hugging my children enough. Don't misunderstand me: I feel I was a good mother; I adored my children and I was affectionate with them. But there were times when I look back now, I know they could have used a hug or a supportive word. I would swoosh them out of the house and tell them to go play because I needed to wax a floor or cook a meal or to do a load of laundry.

It was the '70s, and keeping a clean house and cooking a good meal was top of the list in keeping your man, and being a good wife and mother. I wish I would have sat down and talked to my children about drugs and alcohol, but that was not an important issue where we lived. The mind-set then was only hippies and bums took drugs. And alcohol—what was wrong with that? Didn't everyone drink a little? After all, you need to relax after the daily stresses of life and even though I did not drink, well, it just did not seem an important issue. It was the '70s, and having a drink or so was OK.

Now it is [thirty years later] and I have one son who is a recovering crack addict, and another son who will be going to an alcoholic treatment program. They have spent all their adult life in a haze of alcohol and drugs. I have helplessly watched my children become more and more lost as each year went by. Even though they are trying to get help now, I know they face a lifetime of trying to stay sober.

Maybe, just maybe, if I had hugged them a little more and encouraged them a little more, and warned them that it's just not the hippies and bums who can get entangled in this web of destruction, but also innocent little altar boys who plan to become doctors and forest rangers. If I had done all that, then [today] I would not be writing this.

Jean, 50, real estate broker I am the parent of a special needs child. She is now twelve and has autism and develop-mental delays. My regret is that . . . when she was in the public school system, I wish I did not go along with everything the so-called "professionals" said.

I regret not being more in tune to my child and saying, "No, this is not working and we need to do something else." I guess I went blindly along with many things the school said to do and, looking back, I should have questioned some of the methods they used and recommendations that now I know were not right.

Rick, 33, computer analyst I regret that I did not recognize that a life of abuse was abnormal. It never occurred to me that there was any other way. I knew that there was something wrong, but honestly could not fathom that my rage and fears were anything more than the maelstrom of youth. Now, you may wonder, why is this a regret? For I had no choice as to who my parents were, nor could I have protected myself against the evil that wanders from father to daughter to son as bruises to the skin—and death blows to innocence.

My regret is that I left my four-year-old brother who I had protected and nurtured since his birth, unprotected against the madness when I left to join the Navy. The guilt, shame, and sadness that I feel for this single act of perceived cowardice still makes my eyes well with tears. I love him more than life itself and yet, I left his soul to die at the hands of wolves.

Sharon, 55, in-home caregiver In 1962 my first daughter, Elaine, was born. Her father had been very abusive to me and to her, too, when she was only six months old. I left him, but found I was already a couple of months pregnant again. I did not want another child; Elaine was the only one I wanted. I even had her named when I was only one month pregnant with her.

I carried the second baby full-term, but by then I really knew that I did not want this second child. When Shelley was born, I let one of my sisters take care of her for days on end. I had MY ELAINE, and nothing else mattered. I did not realize that my ignoring Shelley would cause so much pain to her later in life. Even when my girls grew into grammar school, I showed Shelley no attention. Every time Elaine got into trouble by her stepfather, Shelley took the blame. When Elaine got into trouble at school, Shelley took the blame. I thought it was always Shelley getting into trouble.

Both my girls were pregnant before they were married. They are both good mothers. It took me twenty years to realize that I loved Shelley just as much as I did her sister. Elaine told me a few years ago that she was always the troublemaker, not Shelley. Shelley was more thoughtful, calmer, more giving, more generous to her family. She had always thought that she was making mama happy by taking the blame for everything. I wish now that they would have told me the truth about my problem years ago.

My girls are now thirty-six and thirty-seven and they both are the most important people in the world to me. I am the proud grandmother of ten and great-granny of four, but I really do have the enormous ache in my heart for the way I ignored and mistreated Shelley. She is now the most thoughtful, loving person that I know.

Barbara, 47, mom I had a weird dream last night that involved a man that molested me many years ago. That led to regretful thoughts because I didn't confront him or tell my boss at the time. That, in turn, led me to remember another regret from many years ago.

A woman I met through the preschool at Temple Beth-something referred me to a daycare home for Sarah, when she was not even two years old. I checked it out and was impressed by how immaculate the place was, by the schedule that was described to me, and by the ratio of kids to adults.

The first day I got there to pick Sarah up, I was told she had been crying for most of the day. It broke my heart, but I knew she needed to get used to being away from me. The next day, upon arrival, I noticed that all the kids (about five of them) were lined up on a sofa, watching the sixth child play with a toy on the floor. They seemed like they had been scared into behaving in such a patient manner. The kids were all spotless and so was the place. The provider told me they have to take turns. Sarah looked like she had been crying again and started tearing up as soon as she saw me.

In the meantime, I had asked the woman who referred me there how her son was doing. She said she is so happy, because he gets bathed and fed every afternoon, but that he has a horrible rash that doesn't seem to get better.

The third day, when I took Sarah over, a young boy about nine or ten came to answer the door. He should have been in school. When I looked closer, I noticed a big bruise on his jaw and he was holding some ice on it. The provider (his mom) was not in the front room, so I walked further back into the home and found a bedroom with about five cribs crammed in there and babies sleeping or fidgeting—and unsupervised.

I had a combined reaction of surprise at finding infants there (my assumption that this boy had been physically mis-treated), and revulsion at the whole scene. I immediately visu-alized my friend's son getting bathed and having his skin rubbed raw. Even if I was way off base, I knew this was not the place for Sarah. I left with her and never went back.

My regret is not reporting my suspicions and concerns about this place to the proper authorities. I really should have done that. This nagging regret comes back to haunt me every once in a while. I think if I had done what my conscience told me to do, I wouldn't keep having these uncomfortable feelings surfacing when I least expect them. For that matter, the same goes for that slimeball that grabbed me so many years ago.

Ellen, 60, advertising/marketing copywriter I am a sixty-year-old wife, mother, stepmother, and grandmother. I've been married three times. My third marriage has been the longest and has lasted twenty-six years.

When we married in 1973, I was in my early thirties. I had a high-powered, very visible job that gave me a lot of status. I brought two children to the relationship, the product of a nine-year marriage severed by a difficult divorce. He had three older kids from a former marriage. His first wife had died of cancer in 1971. His children were clearly scarred from that event, but we just didn't realize how much. I was a very different woman from the original mother, but thought I could make up for that with my intelligence, good sense, friendliness, and organization. My children seemed to adjust well, but his kids seemed to have a great deal more difficulty.

The strongest regret I have now is that we never thought that the "blended" family needed a lot of help to handle the new situation. (There were just a few books on stepfamilies, and no organizations that we could call on to help us.) Of course, I know the story of the wicked stepmother in *Cinderella*, but later found that almost every culture has a similar story.

In addition, my husband and I had our emotional baggage from our own childhoods. But, in the first flush of our love in 1972, we didn't think about it. My husband and I just went into the marriage very blithely, thinking, "Oh well, we'll just get everybody together, there will be a 'new' mother and father, and everything will be fine." How wrong we were! Although there was some counseling available to grieving spouses at that time, there was none for the children. I believe someone should have recognized signs and symptoms of the maladaptation, but I certainly didn't.

We tried very hard to serve the physical, medical, financial, and growth needs of all seven of us, with mixed results. Now, I sometimes believe that I should have even walked away from the situation, but my husband is a sweet, gentle, generous man and I needed him very much, as he needed me. We are the same religion (he is five years older) and we share many of the same interests. However, I will always wonder how my children might have turned out if I hadn't remarried; my husband sometimes wonders the same, especially since he has had to bear much of the pain of the outcome of our marriage.

Two of his three children (both young women in their thirties) have totally severed their relationship with their father and me, and we are not able to see five of our grandchildren in any open way. No amount of pursuit or the limited psychological help we have managed to get over the years has seemed to matter. The more we try to indicate that the door is open (with the limited contact we have been allowed, along with letters and gifts), the more these two women and their families seem to ignore and even consciously reject us. . . .

The family rift is deep and destructive. The grandchildren are being deprived of knowing a very wonderful grandfather. He believes that when he dies, his children will "dance on his grave." Since I plan cremation for myself, I doubt that will happen, unless they want to dance on the wind and the sea!

Anyway, we have three loving grandchildren whom I do try to enjoy. We have each other, our health, and good jobs. We can travel to beautiful places. I openly tell my other children that I have made many mistakes as a parent, but still love them deeply and try every day to show it, [and] try to be less stressed out as a grandparent than I was as a parent. . . .

I have reunion dreams about my stepkids. We get together with all of our family and say, "Let bygones be bygones. We're all older and wiser and we're parents, too, now, and we understand how much you went through raising five children." But the dialogue is not real; it's only in my head.

The saddest words of all are, "If only I had . . . what might have been." But then I am reminded what a coworker said one day. She said, "Regrets are the cancer of life." And now I believe her!

Scott, 36, advertising executive When I was in the seventh grade there was a girl in my class who was overweight and poorly dressed. She had a very hard time in school and once I saw a group of girls surrounding her and shouting insults. Instead of stopping them, I turned around and walked away. I have, for many years, regretted that I did not walk over and help her. I clearly remember after lunch when we all went back into the classroom, the girl had her head on her desk and was sobbing. I can still hear exactly what it sounded like today.

Name withheld, 26, advertising I like to think of myself as a nice person, thoughtful and kind. However, not one of us is perfect. This imperfection has followed me ever since the dastardly act.

I was only eleven years old and spending the night at a friend's house for a girl's night. We were upstairs in the rec room enjoying ourselves and being goofy. The phone attracted our attention and we decided to do some prank calling. Most of it was harmless: ringing numbers and hanging up.

However, there was a particular girl at my school who was an outcast because of her unusual height and physical maturity—I'll call her Cindy. She wasn't particularly smart and made an easy target. (Kids can be very cruel.) Her phone number was very easy to remember since the last four digits were 0000. My friend and I remembered the unusual number and decided to prank Cindy. When we were sure it was Cindy on the other end of the line we asked her if she "played with herself." At the time I really didn't know what it meant; only heard people talk. Cindy hung up crying and I can still hear her silent response in my head.

I have never since done something so intended to crush the humanity from someone. With all my heart I wish that I could find Cindy and apologize to her. It has stuck with me even if she has been long forgotten. I regret those words and my own insecurities that bred them.

Nicolette, 20, student/mom I regret having really screwed over my first boyfriend four years ago. Sounds rather silly and childish, I know, but it bothers me now even though I am married happily and have an eleven-month-old child. It's not that I hope that if I hadn't screwed him over we'd still be together. I really feel haunted by it (starting to go for his best friend while I still had him on the side); that I hurt them both by tearing their friendship apart.

I was full of myself at the time. I lost a lot of weight in the summer and all of a sudden, guys were paying attention to me. I am sure that had a lot to do with what I did because after it all blew up in my face, it felt like I had to have been out of my mind to twist people's emotions like I did. Karma did work its way back out on me with my next boyfriend and I REALLY deserved it.

Jay, 42, crisis case manager When I was a teenager, I somehow got it into my mind that it was funny and cool to pick on a kid a couple of years younger than me. He was black and it made me feel superior, I guess, to taunt him by yelling out "nigger" every time I saw him. Of course, I only did this in the presence of my friends because those were whom I was attempting to impress.

After several months of this abuse by me, the young boy cornered me in a back alley—alone. I figured we were going to have a pretty big fight, but instead of balling up his fists, he spoke. He told me that what I was doing was cruel, that it hurt, that he had feelings. He said it with a quiet and dignified voice, and his eyes teared up slightly. Then he walked away.

Such shame I felt. Though it happened decades ago, it is the one aspect of my life I would like to erase. What eats at my heart with regret is that I never got the chance to apologize.

Sharron, 46, homemaker My regret is picking on one particular fellow named Arthur. I used to pick on him a lot in high school and now that I've grown up, I regret it. I have tried to locate him to tell him I'm sorry, but never found him.

Paul, 35, disc jockey/record shop manager I'll start with an oldie: when I was about eleven or twelve years old, I was on my way to primary school as this boy from another school cycled past. The boy was a bit younger than me. We always bullied him for having big ears and rather big front teeth and as he drove past, I ran after him and when I caught up with him, I punched him hard on his front teeth (I had an iron key ring on one of my fingers).

I hurt him for absolutely no reason, other than having something to brag about on the schoolyard. The boy drove back to his house and a little while later when I was at the schoolyard, I saw him cycling to his school—with his father's arm around his son's shoulder. I expected the father to come to my school later on to inform my teacher about what I'd done, but he never did.

Years later, always when I saw him passing by, I [wanted] to apologise to him, but to this day I never have. That's also because I moved and, therefore, never see him (pretty lame excuse, isn't it?).

To imagine how scared he must have felt when this ass-hole came running after him for no reason. Why did I do that? I know that I if I see him, I will tell him that I'm not proud of what I've done to him, to say the least.

Mike, 30, Web site manager I'm one of these people in life who is always reflecting on what happened and what might have been. Many friends tell me that it's not healthy to be so retrospective and overanalysing about life: "We must look to the future and not the past" blah, blah, blah.

Yes, yes, I know all that, but I still can't help myself thinking about a girlfriend who I pushed away and destroyed emotion-ally. I am left with an image of her as my ideal future wife. New girlfriends are measured against her and, of course, fail to live up. Consequently, I seem to have a life of successive unfulfilling relationships.

I am a sad bastard. I don't think I'm any different to the vast majority of men in the Western world who have three main areas where they can find happiness:

1) A decent job that they enjoy and are respected at;

2) A wife/partner who they love and who loves them;

3) A group of friends who likes and respects them.

I've come to realise over the years that the lack of just one of these items can be such a cause of unhappiness that it totally overwhelms the others—even if they are fulfilled.

I had a girlfriend called Jackie who was clever, good looking, funny, very affectionate, superb in bed, caring, and loved by my friends and family. She was devoted to me. Strange then, that I broke her heart on three separate occasions. I can still clearly picture the tears starting to run down her face, her eyes desperately scanning mine for any clues that maybe I didn't mean it.

I was so cruel. I can still see the pain and the anguish in her eyes as I took her world from underneath her feet. What I feel such a bastard about is that I never let her believe it was fully over. I would put her world back together again and rebuild this wonderful person who people always commented was such a joy to be around. And then I would take her world apart again.

After much heart wrenching, she took the offer of a job posting abroad and after much consulting with me I said she should go. And she went. I didn't make much effort to keep in touch and she got over me. After this, she never replied to any of my mails. Whether this was because she despised me or it was just her way of looking after herself, I don't know—and probably I never will.

I regret the pain I caused to Jackie. I regret not marrying her. I regret not making enough bloody effort.

Jerry, 47, communications supervisor At the advanced age of eighteen, I only had one thing on my mind—actually three things: sex, drugs, and rock 'n' roll. I was the oldest of five kids—two brothers and two sisters. This regret is concerning the youngest brother.

I had no time for him and failed to see the eagerness in his eyes when we went anywhere together; I failed to feel his admiration of his big brother. I remember the day I took it all away, the day I killed the yearning to be with his big brother. I was going downtown and our mother said, "Take your little brother with you; he so loves you and likes to be with you."

I begrudgingly agreed and loaded the little kid in the car. My frustration with being saddled with this kid came out in a flurry of screams and shouts as we drove down the road. I directed all my adolescent frustrations at this little kid and just broke his heart. He asked me to pull over and got out of the car. He never asked me to take him anywhere again.

I moved out of the house shortly after that and married. I see my little brother once every five to ten years; there is no excitement in his eyes, no recollection of a loving brother. A day never goes by that I don't regret that day in the car, and if I could do any day in my life over, that would be it.

Britt, 29, secretary I regret yelling at my three beautiful children right after I've done it. I look at their angelic faces and realize that my view of them is their view of themselves, and if I am not supportive and kind they think they are bad. They are not. Children are a gift from God and we need to treat them as such—even if they are misbehaving!

My other biggest regret is mistreating a childhood friend in junior high who was one of thirteen children in her family. She didn't have a lot of money or friends, and right when she needed me most, I belittled her and called her names (to impress my friends, I'm sure). I have regretted it since that very day and I hope she has found a way to forgive me.

Daniel, 26, transcriber What I regret the most is letting vulgar, shallow people scare me out of going to school. I came out of the closet very young. Having been raised in an atheist family, I had no idea that the name-calling and constant threats were linked to something much greater than the common cruelty of children. As I became older and entered high school, the threats became more real.

I was cornered by more than thirteen drunken guys in a parking garage at a local mall. My wits and a friend of the family saved me that time. When my parents found out about the incident, it somehow turned out to be my fault. I could have been killed that night had it not been for circumstance. My fear was real, but I let it get the best of me. I let it consume me.

I went to the counselors and told them about my problems and they said that they could do nothing. I stopped going to school for fear that I would be seriously hurt or killed. I dropped out of school after failing tenth grade. I may not be Einstein, but I would never have failed a grade if I had been left alone. That year I let them get the best of me. I don't know what I could have done, short of taking a machine gun to school every day. I just wish that I could have done something to stay in school.

I moved to Colorado. The second week that I was here I was attacked in the street for the same reasons. Although I was terrified, I sent the guy running for his life. Having studied Aikido, Tae Kwon-Do, Qi Gong, and kickboxing, I now consider myself a martial artist. Even though I had a small victory, it doesn't bring back high school and the opportunities that can be forged there. That's why I still regret it.

Kel, 35, artist Although I have helped and loved many animals in my life, I regret deeply treating two or three of God's creatures with cruelty instead of love and compassion. Not only did I deprive myself of their wonderful affection, I created a very painful place in my soul that can never be healed.

Name withheld, 44, artist I had a wonderful friend in high school; she and I went through a lot of stuff together. When she was raped on school grounds, she came to my house first because she was afraid to walk down her street alone. My mother called the police for me.

When she met Herb, she brought him over and I remember the night they got engaged because she came by to show me the ring. I love Kathy like there is no tomorrow and I miss her so.

This is the shameful part: I married in my twenties a man who was opposite of all I was taught was right. In retrospect, I used Don to escape my home life, and my friends did not really care for him. I can't blame that on them because they were right in all kinds of ways.

In June of 1975 I gave birth to my firstborn son and he died soon afterward from various complications. I called Kathy (though I was in shock) and I said something really stupid to her. I said, "You will be happy to know that [our] first child has died." Yes, that is what I said and I did it because she was very open with me that she did not like Don. I hurt her feelings terribly and never heard from her again.

I wrote my story a few years ago to the television show *Reunion* and I actually got a phone call from one of the directors. She told me my letter made her cry and she wanted to do a segment on it. I was thrilled, but before that could happen, the show went off the air.

I don't know what caused me to be such a skunk to a girl that I thought the world of.

Derek, 68, retired I regret that, while my father was alive, I didn't show him the love and respect that he so richly deserved. He was born and was raised in a time when jobs were hard to come by, and those jobs that were to be had, had a low rate of pay.

He had to quit school at an early age to help support his family and yet, despite that, he was a very literate person. As I was growing up, he secured a job as school custodian; this was about 1935 while the effects of the Depression were still very much in evidence in rural America.

I was a complete jerk; never appreciated just how hard he was working, nor did I appreciate the fact that he was able to buy a nice home for us and keep us supplied with all of the material things essential to living.

Dad is, of course, now dead. However, very few days go by when I don't think of him. I wish that I could tell him just how much I regret the way I behaved during those years, when it might have made a difference to him.

Jon, 37, prison caseworker I grew up always loving the Army. I played it endlessly in the wood[s] behind my parents' house. I played with toy soldiers. I made models. I listened to my dad recount his World War II experiences in the Navy.

Needless to say, when I entered college I joined ROTC and the Army Reserve. Fifteen years later I'm still in the Reserve and now a major.

My regret? Twice I had the opportunity to go active duty. I didn't because I was scared, I guess, of leaving home. Life is good for me, but I feel I missed something: to experience independence when it can no longer be found, now that I'm married with a child. What sights and sounds would I have experienced?

Like my father used to tell me, "Everything is for the best."

Name withheld, 49, housewife I regret ever leaving my hometown. I was so tired of it and the job I had that I joined the Navy. I thought I would be taken care of . . . and maybe find a husband. Well, I did find my husband and I got out of the Navy and became a secretary until my first baby was due.

I had a wonderful life with my husband and our three kids until one day, my husband just shut me out. We had been stationed all over the country including Alaska, Hawaii, and Puerto Rico, so I had been through a lot with him. He just basically ignored me except for eating what I cooked and wanting marital privileges. I could not bear for him to touch me the way he was acting and now I regret that.

It has been six years now since I allowed him to touch me. I have gotten very fat and hate myself. My kids have all left home and I just sit at home all day. I started having medical problems because of my weight so I cannot get a job. I just regret my whole life since I left home. I missed growing old with my siblings and my parents, all who are the most wonderful people. Now I am stuck in a loveless marriage, far from those I love.

My advice to anyone reading this is to please be sure whom you are marrying and if he is in the military, you will probably never get to go home again.

Mike, 31, military I'm a single father of a fourteen-month-old daughter. My regret is reenlisting in the military for the third time. If it weren't for the deployments and the long nights away from my family, I probably wouldn't be a single father now. It was a hard lesson to learn, but it has been learned and now I have to worry about not screwing up my daughter's life because of it. The cost of freedom was hard-felt from this end. That is my regret.

Don't get me wrong: I do my job with pride and knowing what I do is worth it. I just think I should of bowed out and let the next man in, stayed home, and been with my family.

Ruthie, 23, student I regret getting out of the military after only eleven months: that was the best and the worst year of my life. I was only eighteen, didn't know what else to do with my life, so I joined the Air Force. My military schooling was a fifteen-month course, but I got sick. I also had a lot of stress, family issues were distracting me, and I started to gain weight. Instead of dealing with these things, I opted to quit.

That was four years ago, and I think about that decision almost every day. I feel like I was thrown off a moving bus and don't know where I am. I tell myself that at the time, there wasn't anything I could do about the situation. I try to forgive myself for being so young and inexperienced with the challenges of life, but it is really hard. I've had panic attacks ever since then, and I can't help but wonder if it's because of my regret. Who knows?

John, 54, self-employed When I was twenty-one I thought I was going to be drafted. It pretty much drove me crazy. I put pressure on my eighteen-year-old girlfriend maybe to marry me (for sure a bad idea at the time) or absolutely to have sex with me (not a bad idea IF she felt willing).

I was very inconsiderate to her and we broke up. I tried, but I could not put it back together. Eventually, as it turned out, I failed my physical because of a bad back. If I could have gone under the assumption that there was practically no chance I would be drafted, I will always wonder what would have happened. I do not know if I could ever make the commitments marriage requires, but it is likely within five or ten years, I would have found out with my former girlfriend.

Hilja, 79, retired seamstress My biggest regret has hung around for more than fifty years. I had joined the Navy Waves intending to be an airplane mechanic. One of the Waves in my group *was* accepted for that purpose, but when I laid it out to our counselor she simply said, "You're too frail." As if she needed proof of her point, I cried (not out loud, just tears).

Without further hesitation she offered the Medical Corps to me and, dumb me, I turned it down! I said I'd be crying over every hurt and sick sailor I saw. So I was sent to Mailman's Training School. It was OK, but her first offer was the perfect one.

Name withheld, 55, retired Thirty-three years ago I joined the Army to fight for this country in Vietnam. I was young and trusted my country and my government. Having been born in 1943 and lost relatives to World Wars I, II, and Korea, I was brought up with a sense of duty to my country.

After Vietnam, I worked overseas in Europe and had the opportunity to become a citizen of a Western European country. I regret today that I didn't. The Europeans may seem screwy to most Americans, but what they do is take care of their own citizens. They don't raise the retirement age of their citizens like this country does. They don't borrow money to give aid to foreign countries with conditions that they use it to buy American goods and services. This is corporate welfare to the rich.

I regret I am American today. This country was once great and had a sense of honesty and decency about it. We have lost it.

Rob, 32, nuclear security officer I served with the First Battalion, Seventh Marines Bravo Company, Third Platoon in Operations Desert Shield and Desert Storm. The biggest regret I have about the war was not finishing the job.

Simple fact: someday in the near future, we will send our young men and women over to where I was—as well as several thousand others—to do a job we should have finished. How will we be able to look at ourselves in the mirror with their blood on our hands and justify it in the end, when in reality, the job should have been finished in 1991?

Please do not make any misunderstandings about what I say; I love this great country of ours and I proudly served it and would have died for it, if need be. But if you're gonna commit to a task that large and lose the lives we lost, don't we owe it to their memory to finish the job?

Jack, 76, semiretired My only regret is that they didn't drop "The Bomb" two years earlier. It would have cut my time in the Southwest Pacific by two-thirds, and would have saved tens of thousands of lives and billions of dollars.

Ray, 68, retired court reporter In 1948 I joined the Marine Corps [and] did not complete high school. I have at times thought that was a mistake, but if I had finished high school, I would probably have been drafted into the Army.

I went to Korea with the first Marine unit to land there in August 1950. The Army was woefully unprepared; all the veterans from World War II were gone. The Marine Brigade was mostly World War II veterans and kids like me were the minority—ergo, we did pretty well. Our casualty rates were much less than the Army. So, though I regretted not finishing school at that time, I probably survived because of it. Who knows? I made it through the Pusan Perimeter, Inchon-Seoul, and the Chosin Reservoir.

My greatest regret is not settling down when discharged and completing my education under the G.I. Bill. I started, but couldn't get my act together. I'm told I have suffered from PTSD [Post-Traumatic Stress Disorder] and still have some problems with it. But I do not regret having served in the

Marine Corps and, from a philosophical point of view, I do not regret having served in Korea. It was the first time we seriously confronted communism and brought their aims to naught. Ninety-eight thousand North Korean civilians voted with their feet and we evacuated them from North Korea when we left. I've since met several of them some forty years later. Of that one thing I am proudest. The terrors of war truly are a sad commentary on humanity, but at least we did one thing worthwhile: saving all those people.

Now, some forty-nine-plus years later, trying to think of "regrets," I'm reminded of a saying I took to heart long ago: never cry over spilt milk. Regrets that weigh on one's mind are a negative and take up too much energy that's better put to other uses.

Chandler, 54, building contractor I graduated from high school in 1961 at the age of sixteen; attended a year of high school postgraduate work because of my age, and in 1962, went off to college at Tulane University where I was enrolled in the [Naval] ROTC program.

My father retired from the Navy that year and was on the faculty there, so the tuition was free. Growing up as the son of a senior naval officer and pilot, I always assumed I would follow in his footsteps. However, I got sick and had to drop out of school for a couple of semesters. My father pointed out that if I joined the Reserves (ideally the Naval Reserves), I would start my longevity early and receive more pay when I finally got a commission.

At the time, 1964, all Reserves required two years active duty—except for the Marine Corps, which required only six months. Therefore, in April 1964, I joined the Marine Corps Reserves with every intention of returning to Tulane and resuming my NROTC program leading to a commission in the U.S. Navy and flight school at Pensacola.

The day of my graduation from Parris Island's Marine Boot Camp was the day of the Gulf of Tonkin incident. That was the first time I heard anything about Vietnam. We were told by our instructors that we were going to war. We were eager and knew we were ready. The Marine Corps gives you nothing if not self-confidence and a belief in the invincibility of the Corps.

After boot camp, I was sent to ITR (Infantry Training Regiment) and ACT (Advanced Combat Training). But when my six months was up, I was sent home to join my Reserve unit and reenroll in college.

Unfortunately, during my active duty, my father had moved to another college and I could not return to Tulane unless I could come up with $3,000 per year tuition. I decided to attend the new college and get commissioned through one of the postgraduation programs. Every few months, at our monthly Reserve unit drills, we were told to get our paperwork up to date, our wills made out, and our affairs generally in order because we would be activated in the near future (such as when [Secretary of Defense Robert] McNamara returned from one of his regular trips to Vietnam), and sent to Vietnam as a unit.

Naturally, we wanted to serve with our buddies and anticipated activation with only a few moans of inconvenience. We were all either in school or employed, and most had families. And we were certainly accustomed to "standing by to stand by"—waiting for word to do something.

Well, about 1967 or so, people began to refer to Reservists as "draft dodgers." Many did try to enlist in the National Guard or other Reserve units to avoid getting drafted and the Reserve units were soon filled to capacity. No more enlistments to the Reserves were accepted unless someone got out.

People of my vintage, Reservists, deeply resented being called draft dodgers since we had joined the Reserves when we didn't have to—and before we ever heard of Vietnam. So, after several years of being told that our unit was going to be activated and it never happening, we told our unit that we were willing to voluntarily go to Vietnam for the thirteen-month tour that was the standard for Marines at that time. We were told that if we transferred to active duty it would have to be for two years: thirteen months in Vietnam and eleven months of barracks duty (KP, guard duty, shine shoes for inspections, etc.).

We said, "Hell no! We will go to Vietnam, but we are way too old and salty to put up with eleven months of make-work barracks duty." Our offer was never accepted.

In 1968 I finished college. By then, the war had turned into a fiasco and we had several years of firsthand reports from Marines returning from Vietnam with stories about how we were not allowed to do what we were trained for and certainly not allowed to win. The Tet Offensive occurred in 1968 and the media reported that we lost the battle and it was another indication of how we had been unable to defeat the VC [Viet Cong] and NVA [North Vietnamese Army] after four years of fighting.

In 1968, I took a job as a financial accountant. In 1970, my six-year enlistment was up and I was discharged from the Marine Reserves. I was never commissioned and I never went to Vietnam. In 1975, I bought a small airport with a few other friends so I could fly when I wanted to.

Now, twenty-nine years after my discharge, I regret not having taken my turn with my contemporaries in Vietnam. I tell myself that had I entered flight school in 1968, I might well not be here now, but I still have a feeling of regret. Whenever I talk with another Marine—or any vet who did go—I have a strong feeling of regret. Should I have made a stronger attempt to do my duty? Should I have gone to flight school? Am I alive today because someone died in my place?

Marvin, 53, small business owner Having regret implies dissatisfaction with a free will choice: I didn't serve in the military by choice. I didn't go to Vietnam by choice. I didn't participate in combat by choice. I didn't end up with really nasty, lingering problems by choice.

Regrets? How can you regret something you didn't want or choose? There was no choice—only Uncle Sam with the threat of prison if I didn't go. We were the unwilling doing the unnecessary for the ungrateful.

I chose to let Uncle Sam enslave me rather than choosing to flee the country. With 20/20 hindsight, I maybe ought to regret that choice. And to be honest, I wouldn't want to regret going, but my present life probably would have been a hell of a lot better if I hadn't gone. I probably wouldn't be concerned that my ability to work—ever again—may be ending because of 'Nam.

William, 35, computer technician I met Teri at a weird time in my life. We took to each other almost instantly and became inseparable. I decided to join the Army and she was all behind the idea. I thought it was a good way to make a living and to take care of my dependents (we didn't know yet that there was no way we could have children).

Things went fine through basic [training], got interesting during jump school (I threw my hip out, an injury which bothers me still), and I ended up in Germany. My father and my uncles had served in the Army and had all been to Germany. As a child, you can imagine all the stories I'd heard of how cool and beautiful the country was. During my tour in Germany, my wife developed medical problems [and] went to the clinic in Nuremberg to get [them] taken care of. They told her it was a yeast infection. Neither of us took notice that they kept saying that for over a year. They just kept saying, "Infection this and infection that."

She developed another problem with abdominal pains

and had to be taken by ambulance to a German hospital. There, the doctors immediately noticed something wrong and did a biopsy. It came back cancerous. The "infection" diagnosed by Army doctors for almost two years was cancer of the vulva. A full hysterectomy was done for the abdominal pains (the pain in her abdomen was actually a set of badly infected and now useless ovaries—totally missed by Army doctors), along with a vulvectomy (total removal of the vulva, including the clitoris). The operation was so drastic, she developed mental problems, including a pretty strong suicidal urge. She went through treatment in Germany, but the medical facilities were not geared for in-house treatment of dependents with mental problems, or so we were told.

I managed a compassionate reassignment back to the States a short time after she got interned in a mental hospital in Florida. I was eventually sent to Ft. Benning, Georgia, and she followed shortly to another mental facility in Columbus. Then, the allocation for dependent mental health ran out and she was going to be sent to the Georgia State Mental Hospital. The people she was in the Columbus facility with filled her head with how bad the state facility was. She lied her way out of going by telling the staff she no longer wanted to kill herself.

Things got a little rocky between us; you can imagine the problems after such a radical operation. The end came one weekend when she looked good enough to take a trip by herself to see her family in Orlando. We had just gotten the car we had purchased in Germany and it was running good; I didn't see any reason she should not go. She left Thursday night [and] I got a call about 04:00. She had stopped, got a beer in a convenience store, and had one on the way along with the usual battery of antidepressants. She dozed at the wheel and totaled the car.

I went and picked her up (bailed her out actually; she had been arrested and booked for DUI). Saturday, my parents were in town to see me and lo and behold, I was called in for an alert. I got cut loose around 16:00 [and] went to see my parents along with my uncle-in-law (also stationed in Ft. Benning). I got invited to the NCO club by my uncle and went home to change. I needed some time to get my head right after having to bail my wife out. I went to the club with my uncle and got home around 01:30 on Sunday. When I got home, my wife had committed suicide with all the pills she had been given by the Army mental health staff.

I've never regretted my service to my country. I regret that I paid for my service with an innocent life.

Robin, 55, (no occupation given) I left my home, mother, half-sister, and stepfather after my senior year of high school and entered the Naval Academy, completely unprepared mentally OR physically for the next four months. It was a nightmare I relive and regret almost daily, even now, at fifty-five.

My dear grandpa secured an appointment for me and I let him down when I washed out. I let me down by going at all. When I went for my physical, the Navy enlisted men let me pass, but I could not even do one of the required ten pull-ups or other tasks to their proper levels. This was not right of them; it was not right of me to be so unfit, but I didn't know any better. I was just looking for a free education, I suppose, or maybe to please the family. I don't remember. I wish I had never heard of that torture chamber.

About the fifth day there, life as I knew it—decent life— was forever ended. I was constantly sleep-deprived for the next four months. Days began for us on the "weak squad" at 5 A.M.: PT [Physical Training] for an hour followed by another half-hour of regular PT and another hour later in the day. I was exhausted constantly, stressed beyond my limits. For fun, the upperclassmen would harass us with "come-arounds."

"Come around Mr.—and be wearing seven sets of sweat gear." I had one set. I had to borrow the rest, and you can imagine what the folks I borrowed from felt toward me: HATE. I also had to wear seven plastic raincoats. Another come-around was to bring ten mattresses down several flights of stairs. Those classmates really hated this one, too. I had to make all their beds up, but wasn't very good at that and they got in trouble through me.

And so it went, day after day. I pleaded with my family to let me apply to leave, but they told me to hang in there. I knew they were wrong. I regret having to ask their permission. I regret ever seeing them again, to be honest. It got worse, and I finally did get their permission and left and went home.

But it never was home again; something happened to me that nothing could heal.

The depression began there. One thing I read was that stress could trigger a dormant gene and cause depression. I think that is what happened. I get a small disability income now. I had over seventy-two jobs and lost them to the illness. I have been hospitalized over twelve times. Someone should have seen, but there was no one on my side. I regret being born now. I regret the time spent there. I regret having to ASK permission to leave and not getting it when it might have mattered, before I was damaged so. I regret 1963 and every year since, and wish I had run away from home in 1962.

I regret especially hurting my grandpa who just loved me and I let him down. I'm sorry, grandpa; I wasn't up to that place. You couldn't have known. I couldn't have known, either, but there was no one who did know and I regret that the most.

Hollis, 51, war-disabled My regret is not shooting the s.o.b who said, "You won't regret it."

Name withheld, 35, self-employed Seventeen years ago, I entered a prestigious college with scholarships and high hopes. Three years later, I left a courtroom a convicted drug felon. I have spent the last fourteen years of my life dealing with that. Literally.

I spent not a day in prison or jail. My probation officer was a truly saintly man who recognized that my punishment would come not in a jail cell, but through my own eventual recognition of what wreckage I had made of my own life. He took pity on me and spared me the further humiliation of spending a month in jail, and talked the judge into suspending my sentence.

Lucky break? Maybe.

Not a day goes by that I don't confront what I did and what my actions did to my potential. Regardless of the fact that I ultimately graduated and that I now run a successful small business, I am a drug felon. Regardless of how much money I earn and how many professional successes I achieve, I am a drug felon. Two words characterize me.

I don't advertise my conviction, but I can't deny it, as it is a matter of public record. While I may argue that mine was a victimless crime (a matter between me and my own body), the courts have left me with certain "disabilities" that, unless and until I am granted a pardon by the governor of that state, will remain with me until my death.

Regardless of what you think of a particular law or how little respect you may have for it, my advice to you is: if you choose to violate a law, be prepared to pay the price for it for the rest of your life. If you are not so prepared, you will have regrets.

Kenny, 24, inmate/assault III What I regret more than any-thing in my life of twenty-four years has to be when I let alco-hol and the fast life take number one priority over my family, school, and sports. I painfully remember all the camping trips, vacations, dinners, and movies I would turn down because drinking was more important. I painfully remember all the college classes and baseball practices I would stumble into, drunk. And as I sit here in the penitentiary, I realize how special and loving my family is and nothing can tear apart the bond of a loving, supportive family.

Rae, 37, photographer My husband was incarcerated and he served two-thirds of his sentence of ten years. He came home to a stable home, a family, started a business, went to work every day, [and] we attended church. He complied with all of the conditions of his release. However, the New York State Division of Parole had a different opinion.

Over the years (I am a photographer), I have collected various nude photographs of myself and had maybe seven or eight photographs that included my husband. Four [New York State] parole officers came into my home three months after my husband's release, handcuffed him in the living room, and lead him into our bedroom. They searched the bedroom; they searched my dresser (although I emphatically objected to their search of my property). They found in my dresser photographs of my husband and I engaging in marital relations.

They confiscated the photographs and forty-five days later, while my husband was in jail, they charged him with possession of pornography. They sentenced him to two years (which he is now serving).

I have many regrets. I guess the first would be to have be-lieved that I could have faith that the U.S. Constitution would protect my rights to be free of unreasonable search, and to have some expectation of privacy in my own home. I never waived those rights. And there isn't one governmental agency that will assist me. I regret being naive, to think that the sys-tem that is in place to uphold the law couldn't break the law under the guise of protecting us everyday citizens, but they do. I regret ever having lost the faith in our government that was instilled in me as a small child.

I regret having to go through another two years of hell while he is incarcerated over something so trivial—trivial in the scope of crime that has run rampant in our society. My husband took two photographs of me; I took the remainder or had them taken over the years. If they were so criminal, why wasn't I charged?

Tucker, 37, masonry contractor At the age of twenty, I was convicted of armed robbery in California. While incarcerated, I picked up another assault charge and ended up in San Quentin and later, after my custody level dropped, was transferred to Soledad—a couple of the tougher prison mainlines to walk.

For anyone to think that it was the serving of the time that caused any regret, I will only tell you that prison taught me harsh lessons, but none of those lessons were about re-gret. They were about hate, anger, fear, and my first experience with rampant, or at least, overt racism.

I can think of more things I regret *not* doing than the things done. After spending time listening to men swap lies on the yard, I decided that phrases like "should have, could have, and would have" were not going to be the litanies of my life. Now I feel the same about "should not have" or "I would not have, except. . . ." Those phrases are not the litanies I want for my life, either.

Often, it seems that the most profound mistakes are the things that give a person dimension. It seems even more likely that it is our mistakes that teach us empathy for others. Success crowns us and allows us pride, but for me, it is the pain of my mistakes and errors that has taught acceptance of the mistakes of others.

Strangely, I do regret committing the crimes, but the experience of having paid for them with five years of my life I do not regret. It was in prison and on parole where I really experienced the worst and the best of others and myself.

I can only believe that I am a summary of my experiences and that changing any of those experiences may change the me of today. As a result, I am not sure that I would be all too willing to change any of them.

Lynne, 31, X-ray technician My biggest regret was falling in love with a man who spent most of his adult years in prison. [I] met this man while he was in prison, overlooked the fact that he has done wrong, figured he just made a mistake—a bigger one than most of us, but nonetheless, a mistake.

I gave this man my heart, two years of my life waiting for him to be released and lots of money—ashamed to divulge how much. He led me to believe that he loved me. His kindness and sweetness made me fall in love with him; I would have done anything in my power to help him in any way I could.

I regret letting him know just how much he meant to me and how much I cared for him. He made me a lot of empty promises, took advantage of my feelings for him. I gave him patience and understanding; all he gave me was some time. After all, he had plenty of it to spare.

He was released last fall, spent two weeks with me and I had a glorious time, fell even deeper in love with him. Then all of a sudden he disappeared and I never heard from him for a couple of months. He was back on the inside and apparently had lost my number. I had to believe him. After all, I felt he had never held anything back from me.

He charmed me again for a few months before letting me know that he could be released out on bail with only a few hundred dollars. I gave him the money. I missed him so much and needed to be near him.

Two weeks after that I went to visit him and found out that the person who visited him before me signed in as his girlfriend, [and I] was taken advantage of again. I believe there are a few convicts that are reformed and trustworthy, but most of them cannot be trusted; they use and take advantage of people. Maybe it's because they've been away from people who care, they have no clue what to do.

If I had to do it all over again, [I] would never give my heart to anyone who isn't able to give half as much as he's able to receive.

Joyce, 36, waitress My biggest regret in life is letting a controlling husband get me addicted to drugs. The drugs contributed to crime. Prison is not a place for anyone, especially a female. I now have a wonderful husband (Thanks, Bubba) who has really contributed to the changes in my life.

To all you young adults: stay in school. DO NOT EVEN TRY DRUGS! This regret of mine could save your life!

Name withheld, 52, corrections I regret nothing. The best decision I ever made was to go into law enforcement. I have been a LEO (Law Enforcement Officer) for thirty-three years and I do not regret a minute of that decision. As a LEO, I get to help people who really need help. I have the honor of protecting my fellow citizens from predatory criminals who prey on my friends and fellow citizens. Being a Law Enforcement Officer is the most rewarding thing that I can do with my life.

While surfing the Net one Sunday, I discovered Restitution Incorporated, a nonprofit organization "dedicated to promoting healing between offenders and victims," according to their Web site, restitutioninc.org.

Part of the site features artwork for sale that's created by Death Row inmates, with proceeds earmarked for victims' families.

In the case of inmate Harvey Green, the families declined the money, so he offered it to PROUD (Personal Responsibility to Overcome with Understanding and Determination), based in Durham, North Carolina. PROUD helps prevent at-risk children from committing their first crimes, and also helps keep court-referred juveniles from becoming repeat offenders.

One of PROUD's staff members asked Harvey to write a letter to the teenagers studying conflict management. His letter was read aloud to the class.

Harvey, 38, Death Row inmate My name is Harvey Green. To most and probably all of you, it means nothing. But to the State of North Carolina it means that I'm a murderer, a killer, and a menace to society. A man without hope or any redeemable qualities.

I must confess that I have killed two people, but I am not as the State of North Carolina makes me out to be. If the truth will be known, I started out like most of you.

I grew up in the country in a farming community surrounded by people who loved and cared for me. I was a quiet child; never one to get in trouble, that is, until I started hanging out and drinking wine and smoking grass. I felt that my parents and most grownups didn't even see me or know what was happening, and my friends were no help—if anything, we kept each other in booze and drugs. At this time, drugs weren't as visible on the streets as they are now and rock cocaine did not even exist.

I figured that my life would change when I joined the Army, but no, it didn't, and I found that drugs were just as plenteous there. Why did I do drugs? I did them not only to get away from my problems, but also as a way to deal with my problems. Well, in 1982, alcohol and drugs gave me a long time in prison: a year and a half in the stockade in Fort Leavenworth. While there, I had plans to live right once I got out, but the plans still included my use of drugs and alcohol.

I got out in 1983, and while looking for a job I was still using and drinking. It had gotten to a point where I would lie to get what I wanted. It even got so bad that to eat and continue my lifestyle, I stole and forged checks from my father and not too long after that, I had killed two people during a botched robbery attempt.

I was tried and sentenced to two counts of death. Stop and think about that word. Just think about it. Now think about your mother, father, family, friends—the people you care about and love. Just think . . . take your time . . . never, ever seeing them again.

No, all of you weren't even born yet when my life, as most people knew it, ended when the prison doors of Central Prison here in Raleigh closed behind me. Yes, I'm not too far from any of you, but yet, it is as if I'm millions of miles away. I know that some of you think prison is easy, that nobody can tell you what to do or say. Well, my friends, it isn't so.

You think prison is easy! How many of you have ever walked in fear for your life? Or seen a friend dying because he stood up when he should have shut up because nobody was going to tell him what to do?

I see through the eyes of a real old man and I know the environment I'm in. Stabbings and killings used to be the normal things in here on a daily basis. The guards don't care what happens to you; they just want to go home in one piece and with their lives.

Imagine your mother or father dying and you can't go to the funeral because the State is scared that you'll attempt to escape. It happened to me when my father died. That is a feeling that you don't wish upon your worst enemy. Prison isn't a glamorous life that the videos and rap say it is. It is a real world of men preying on other men's fear to show that the fear they have doesn't exist.

The State plans to murder me in less than a month to say that killing is wrong. I look back upon my life and I can see that there were many people there ready to help me, but I didn't need help because I knew what was going on. Oh, how wrong I was.

In the quiet of night, you can hear grown men crying because they want out of here and they finally understand that this isn't the life they thought they wanted, and they know that they should have listened to the people who tried to help them.

All of you are in a unique situation now and you may not know it. Look at the people who take the time to steer you away from this all, not because they have a job or they have to, no, it is because they care and love each and every one of you and don't want you [to] become a person who is on the road that I, and others before me, were on: a road of destruction. . . .

You all are my future—my hopes and dreams—and I pray that you all will never darken a prison door, for if you do, it only gets darker and darker as you try to survive. Oh, I know that some of you don't believe me, but remember, I've been your age and experienced what you're going through, but none of you have reached my age or the experiences I have been through.

This world and this State don't care a thing about you and is most happy that people go to prison and they stay in prison. I haven't even begun to tell you of the other horrors, but due to your ages, it is unsuitable.

You are told when to sleep, get up, eat, work, play, and where to be, and that's only if you have some kind of move-ment. Now comes visiting day, when you may or may not get a visit from your family or friends. People will forget about you and you may not see your family for years at a time.

I was hardheaded and wouldn't listen and I ended up here in prison and on Death Row, waiting to be killed by the end of this month if the Lord doesn't stop it. Am I happy? No! Do I love and miss my family? Yes! Could I have prevented this? Yes! What can you to do avoid this? Stay in school, don't join gangs, leave the guns and drugs alone, and most of all, if you feel that people don't understand you or that you need someone to talk to, talk to friends you can trust. Support one another, confide in parents and teachers, your Sunday school teacher or minister, and always take the time to weigh your choices.

And don't let anyone force you to do something you don't want to do.

Look at my life as a guide how not to do things and only look at the positive to help yourself. I've seen and talked to many young men in here from Durham-Raleigh and through-out North Carolina. Maybe some of them you have known all your life and the first thing they said is, "This isn't how I thought it would be or how I heard or seen about it through music or on TV." Then, most of them want to go home after the first day or two. Guess what? They can't! This isn't a game! This is all too real.

I feel terrible how I put my mother and family as well as the victims' families through all the pain and anguish, and I now know that it's going to get worse. How can your mother and father stand by and see you killed or when the judge gives you time to serve? I pray and hope that none of you will ever see that day.

Regardless of what I tell you or convey about prison life, some of you will test it, but the final choice is yours! Always yours.

Harvey was executed September 24, 1999.

chapter 7

The Dark Side

Who against hope believed in hope?

—Romans 4:18

I won't lie to you: this is the most troubling section in the book. It contains eleven accounts of abandonment, neglect, abuse, addiction, poverty, violence, and cruelty—some more traumatic than others.

These stories are included not because of their shock value, but because each person's story, with few exceptions, illustrates a basic human trait: survival.

Somehow, these people persevere—albeit damaged—despite their often tragic circumstances. Wrapped around their regrets are, in several cases, remarkable acts of survival that defy all odds. And that's what impressed me the most.

Are any of them heroes? If you define "hero" as one who

shows amazing courage, then the answer is a resounding "Yes."

But sadly, I received even more heartbreaking tales than you see here. I chose these specific stories as stark reminders of just how manageable life is for the majority of us—and how often we fail to realize it.

One participant named Jim put it in perspective when he wrote: "*In all honesty, the thing that keeps me going is the fact that no matter how much I regret, there are so very many who have it so much worse than I do. Compared to many of them, I'm in a relative paradise.*"

♦ ♦ ♦

Suzanne, 39, formerly homeless I was locked up when I was twelve to fourteen years old, lived on the streets, in fact. Grew up on skid road in Portland [Oregon] from age fifteen to eighteen, more or less back in the days when there was [*sic*] no women or white women there.

I have had a husband in prison. I now write many incarcerated people in many states: a black gang member in California; a so-called leader of the Dixie Mafia in Florence [Colorado]; and another man in Mississippi that used drugs and sexually assaulted his stepdaughter, all kinds of them.

I don't work, am on SSI. One thing about us who were locked up at an early age: we didn't learn how to work, we can't hold a job, and those who are antisocial or who exhibit such behavior or a crime-filled life, don't have an occupation.

I consider myself lucky to have what I have and to have this wonderful tool to reach out to mostly the upper classes and educate them or inform them about life on the downside. Most are shocked, and there are few like me online—a few, not many. My boyfriend is Mexican from Mexico; a good, kind man who bought me this computer so I could learn and pass the time while he works.

As for me, well, I had the chance to go to college and I blew it. I took the love I had for granted, and then poof—it was gone. If I had only known that mothers don't always love their daughters no matter what. If I had only known how weak my mother was and that when my boyfriend who was twenty-three would come calling on me and find me gone; that with his charms of a pedophile and a sick, sick man, he would woo her ... and off they would go and my life would change forever.

I thought it was cool and fun to party and do as I pleased. But then, when I could, when she said, "OK, you want to party, go ahead," things changed. They moved and left me in the streets where I was raped and had VD and lice.

I was locked up for six months for nothing [but] being unwanted. It was called "beyond parental control." I was hand-cuffed, feet cuffed, and shuffled on to be locked up in Nashville. They made us with VD sit on a towel for two weeks everywhere we went, "so no one else wouldn't catch it," they said. These were nurses.

'Course the south is twenty years behind the times, always will be. Life rolled on and I found myself in a world where I was not mature enough to handle, and so what I regret is not going to school, for running away and for being so wild. I could have done so much with my life, if only I didn't run away [and] sleep with men from the halfway houses. I never had a father, maybe that's why.

Thinking I was invincible is my regret. I was beautiful and thin and now I am old and fat, lost all my teeth and am sick. Those are real consequences to my actions that can never be changed. It's a miracle I am not in prison myself.

Some of us are in prisons without walls. And I am one.

Dave, 23, student I regret not confronting my mother about why she left our family. I was only ten, and really didn't understand the complexity of her leaving. To me, it was just mom and dad don't get along, so they are getting a divorce. Over the years, I have grown to understand that mom left for what I see as selfish reasons, and I haven't quite figured out how to deal with the corresponding emotions.

Mom may have left us to be with one of her college history professors. Maybe because she didn't want the responsibility of her kids; maybe because she got married to her first husband at eighteen and never really got to be a kid—or a combination. I really think mom left because it is much easier to quit and start over than to fix what is broken.

You see, my half-sister (from my mom's first marriage) and my dad were in counseling due to dad having dictator-ish control issues. One day mom starts crying and says, "He does the same things to me!" OK, so the hammer hits my dad and he concedes he had controlling issues. He commits to work on it and commits to make his marriage work.

I think for my mom, admitting that there was a problem was a huge deal, in and of itself. For her, the marriage was over the second the veil of illusion fell. Mom was unwilling to work through their marriage problems and left within a month. I remember helping her unpack boxes in the morning at her new place, before she took me back to my home for my birthday party. My half-sister has told me that mom may have been dating the history professor before the divorce went through. It wouldn't surprise me if he were one of the contributing factors that accelerated the end of mom and dad's marriage.

I do know that mom had sex with him in Motel 6's all across the country during a road trip in the summer when I was thirteen. I know, because I was in the same room, five feet away, pretending to be asleep. I regret not saying something then.

What really whacked me out was he has the same name as I do. Imagine hearing your mom having sex, calling out your name. It was hard enough being thirteen, bursting with hormones; I didn't need the insinuation of an Oedipus complex. I regret the blunted intimacy I have due to that trip and I regret not doing something to stop it. During the sex, I just laid in bed, praying for it to end soon. I just pretended like it didn't happen. I just went along with it because everything was OK.

She lived with and eventually married the history professor. Funny thing is, her life with him isn't much different from her life with my dad. He is controlling just like my dad can be: he has to drive everywhere and his needs come first—yadda, yadda, yadda.

OK, so now she had a Master's Degree (ironically, in history) and she [just] watches baseball on TV. She got her education at the expense of our family and she does nothing with it. The biggest difference I see between her life with my dad and her new life is she got the chance to avoid her parental responsibilities to her kids. I regret not being able to be an adult and deal with my mom and the feelings I have toward her.

When I was a teen, I used the excuse that she was the adult and she should have to come to me. What I didn't know then was my mom lives in a fantasy world where everything is OK, and we all just have to get along. Now, as a young adult, I have come to grips with the reality that I am more mature than my own mother.

I regret the fear that I have toward confronting my mother—the fear that she won't love me anymore if I dig up old hurts. I regret not being able to see that, at best, my mother and I have a strained relationship, and confrontation can do little harm. I regret the little pretend hugs I get every holiday. I regret not confronting my mom with the truth: the truth of how I have cried myself to sleep, of how I have lost intimacy with my girlfriends, of how self-destructive I have behaved in the past.

I regret the gut-wrenching emotions I feel whenever I hear someone talking about how mothers always love you—and how they won't hurt you. I regret the loss of illusion. I miss having an honest relationship with my mom. Above all, I regret that I am as much to blame for the current state of affairs as she is.

Now that I have written this, I know what I have to do next.

Raymond, 52, hairdresser I had so many regrets. They go back to when I was thirteen years of age. I was in the Scouts at the time of the incident. I had always felt out of sync with the fellows that I went to school with. I had always tried to find ways to fit in; scouting was one of the ways I did it.

One night the scoutmaster (a man of fifty-two and married) made sure I was the last one to be dropped off. We all lived up in . . . the country. As we drove up the narrow, dark, country road, he turned up an old logging road. Questioned about where we were headed, he laughed and said, "You will see."

Finally, he stopped and gave me a choice: "You can get out and find your way home or. . . . "

His hand then reached over and he put it in my crotch. I was frightened by the dark and did not know what to do. I also was very shy and withdrawn; you might say I was timid. Anyway, after the rape I was taken home and it was repeated twice more before I could convince my dad that I just didn't fit in with the Scouts.

My regret is that I was too scared to tell anyone. Who could I turn to? That one act took me thirty years to recover from. I went through so many adversities, yet I finally woke up. I fought and I learned and I finally knew there is nothing wrong with me, just the circumstances I chose for my life's lessons.

Mat, 34, writer My biggest regret is drinking. I drank for eleven years. I don't regret the damage I did to my body and the crazy things that happened anywhere near as much as all of the time I wasted. Sitting in a bar, all day, every day. The people were nice enough, but all there was to talk about was television and sports. Hours and hours sitting, anesthetized, doing nothing. Staying in my little apartment drinking, staring at a wall.

I regret the time wasted more than anything. Couldn't I have at least written something or made paintings or taken up a hobby? No. I just pissed away eleven years drinking. Anything I accomplished in that time period was almost out of the inevitable inertia of living. I didn't lift a finger to do anything, but twist off the beer bottle top.

Mark, 41, information technology consultant Boy, Barry, you don't have a clue, do you? I have few regrets anymore; used to have lots, but I took care of those once I was sober. When AA's get sober we GET our second chances. There is some melancholy involved when relationships can't be mended or people died before we had a chance to tell them we love them.

Many of us have even ended up in prison for murder or vehicular homicide. But we move past our regrets. It would be a good lesson to teach in your book.

And alcoholism is more of a blessing than a curse—but definitely not a regret. It's not something I DID, how can it be a regret? You're trolling the wrong newsgroup, kiddo.

[Later that day, Mark added this follow-up:]

The reason I came off harsh—and I hope I did—is that alcoholism is a VERY misunderstood disease. Even today, when Lifetime Television has some movie about addiction every other week, and half the sitcom characters are recovering something-or-others.

I do not—make that *cannot*—regret alcoholism. Alcoholism is not something that I did to myself; it is a disease.

And regrets will kill an alcoholic. Through twelve-step recovery programs, we learn to come to terms with our past, make amends, and move on. If you define regret as something you would go back and change if you had the chance, few alcoholics with any sobriety have regrets. Regrets, by definition then, would be living in the past—and we have to live in the present.

When I was drinking, I understand that I was physically abusive. I'm told that I beat my son while in blackouts. Today, as a means of repairing the damage, I take him to Al-Anon and spend more time with him than most dads do with their sons. No regrets.

Name withheld, 22, student I have a regret that nothing can ever come close to. Regardless of whatever else I have done in the past or whatever else I do in the future, this will always be my biggest regret.

I grew up in a well-respected home. My family was dubbed the "Mexican Brady Bunch." We went to church every Sunday and both my parents even became preachers. I was the only girl and the youngest in the family. So, as you can imagine, very spoiled and happy.

I met my boyfriend when I was in the seventh grade. I loved him immediately, [but] it took him five years before he saw me as more than a friend. I knew sex was a "sin" and when I was a child, had sworn I would keep my virginity until I was married. When my boyfriend and I made love for the first time, I felt guilty, but knew I was deeply in love and that we didn't just have sex. I was twenty years old.

A year later I became pregnant. Scared and worried about my family's reaction, I decided abortion was the answer. My grandmother was a pastor of a church; my parents [were] also very important in the church district. I could not stand to have to tell my daddy that his little girl was going to have a baby.

My boyfriend, who is pro-choice, stood beside me the whole way. He never stopped loving me for killing his child, just held my head when I cried; helped me to breathe when I didn't have a will to. My family never found out about the pregnancy and the abortion.

Today, my child would have turned one. We would have had a huge birthday party. Everyone would have been there, loving my child and myself. What would have been hard to deal with at first, would have been OK in the long run. This incredible blessing that was given to me, I killed. I have to deal with that every day of my life.

This is my one and only regret: never giving my child the chance to live because I was too selfish. I thought I was "too young," "couldn't afford it," "What about school?" I asked my boyfriend last week what his regret was: he said it was getting me pregnant.

Mine is not letting the baby live.

Jeanette, 33, administrative technician My biggest regret in life is growing up too fast. I was fifteen years old and thought I knew everything. I got pregnant a month after my

"Sweet 16" birthday. My son was born with Cerebral Palsy. He is unable to walk. He uses a wheelchair or scoots around on his bottom. At the age of sixteen, he still wears diapers.

I remember, before I turned seventeen, I was half a million dollars in debt with medical bills for him. I really regret getting pregnant at such a young age and sometimes I'm angry with myself for getting pregnant.

My son's father was a very abusive man. He used to tell me how fat and ugly I was and how lucky I was to have him because who would want a fat and ugly girl like me with a retarded kid. Because I thought I was so grown up and knew everything, I cheated myself out of my youth. I never got to experience prom, graduation, or just being a carefree teenager. I was too busy taking care of a disabled baby/child/ teenager.

I am now thirty-three and my son is sixteen. I am currently unemployed. I lost my job when my niece decided to live her own life. (She was helping me care for my son.) If I continue to work, then I would have to earn enough to pay someone $6.50 to $11.50 an hour to care for my son. Having a job that would pay me that good so I could pay someone to care for my son, is out of the question.

Just so my son can qualify for SSI and the Oregon Health Plan, I must maintain my monthly income at a certain level. If I make too much, then the State and other agencies say I am over income and I won't get any help. Though I currently receive some help through the State, it isn't enough. I've had to turn down raises numerous times and I've had to ask my employer to pay me less than what the job offered.

Right now, my son is on the waiting list to be placed out of home. I regret I can't take care of my son. He didn't ask to be born and he didn't ask to be born disabled. I didn't ask for a disabled child. I regret having to place my son out of home. One minute I'm fine with the idea and the next I'm depressed. I've gone through every imaginable emotion on this.

If I could turn back the clock I would have studied hard in high school, remained a virgin, [and] got to know the kids that were involved with the school, instead of hanging around all the losers and druggies.

I can only tell my story in hopes that if [other teenagers] are going down the path I took, [they] can read how my life has been and how hard it still is now, and [they can] turn their life around and lead a productive, positive life.

Then what I've gone through wasn't in vain.

Ashley, 33, administrative assistant I regret showing kindness, love, and compassion to a fifteen-year-old boy named Matthew when I was nineteen years old. I regret instilling in him the belief that he could become whatever he wanted to be, wishing him success and happiness when we parted ways. How could I have possibly foreseen that he would come to have an obsession about me, which came to light in 1994?

From 1993 to 1998 Matthew stalked me, harassed me at work, broke into my home several times [and watched] me sleep. But the most horrific act he committed was in 1997: Matthew drugged and raped me.

By 1999, I suffered from a nervous breakdown; I put a noose around my neck (I've not told anyone about this). It's funny how your body reacts when it recognizes it's about to be destroyed. Instead, I opted to seek the assistance of the chaplain at my church.

Every day, I wish to God I'd never met Matthew. For how could someone, who once claimed to be my soul mate, cause me to go through so much hell? I have trouble concentrating. I used to be so quick and friendly in communicating with people. My family doctor has diagnosed me with Post Traumatic Stress Disorder. I've been to the emergency room a couple of times, thinking I was about to die of a heart attack or had developed diabetes.

Matthew has ruined my life. At thirty-three, my hopes of having a family are all but diminished. I doubt I could ever trust another person. He has taught me that I have poor judgment about another person's character. And will I ever show kindness, love, or compassion for another living soul? Not on this planet.

I find it unusual that Matthew is no longer so "interested" in my life, ever since I begged mutual acquaintances to make him leave me alone. I think he ought to know the damage his recent actions have done: for all of you rapists out there, or anyone who tramples on the emotions of another, your insidious crimes spread hatred like an evil disease—to not just your victims, but to everyone.

Not only have my creditors experienced a loss (for six months I was unable to work), but so have my family, my friends, my neighbors. All those that I touch or may have touched because now, there's one less kind soul in the universe who used to love to make people laugh.

So, for the criminals, as you sit alone in your bedroom and wonder why? Well, it's because one too many angels have bitten the dust.

Thelma, 53, retired I regret being born; my life has been very, very miserable. My father told my mother that I wasn't his and forbid her to bring me home from the hospital. Instead, her mother took me—my grandmother. She was an alcoholic and a very violent person.

I am legally blind and she never validated anything that I accomplished in life. Her favorite words to me were, "You ain't shit, you will never be shit, you will never have shit!" This has had a negative effect on me all of my life.

When I was nine, my mother died. My grandmother made a death promise to her that she would raise the rest of my sisters and brothers. This was a terrible mistake because my grandmother resented this promise. We eight kids heard about it every day of our lives, until we were old enough to leave the nest.

Meanwhile, there was also my aunt in the mix, who was my mother's younger sister, and the second daughter of my grandmother. My aunt didn't want us around because she felt that we were robbing her of all materials in life, because there were so many of us. She also constantly inflicted pains of words daily.

We had a truly, wildly, interrogating, disruptive, violent-beatings-until-the-blood-ran life. Because of this, I married the wrong men. Life was even worse with them. It was like I married my grandmother and aunt. I've had many, many struggles and twist and turns through the road of life. . . .

My income is so minute, I can't afford to buy groceries oftentimes. I have never had any relationship where the person was interested in me as a person. No, their only interest was to use me in some way! I am not validated as a person by anyone! Imagine that! This is my lot in life and I didn't ask to be here! I spend many lonely hours, days, months, and years.

To add icing on the cake, I was even born the wrong race. No matter what I might accomplish in life, I will never be validated because I am black. Imagine traveling with other blind people who think they are better than me, simply because they are white. Imagine ophthalmologists [who] refuse to lay claim to your optical diseases because you are black.

I had to take Social Security to court to get disability benefits. There were twenty-one pieces of evidence that showed that I was legally blind from birth, yet they kept turning me down for benefits. Even the blind agencies treat us different from the whites. I am sitting here typing this with no talking software. If I was [sic] white, Blindness and Visual Services would have bought it for me, since I can't afford to buy the necessary software and equipment.

No, I am not rolling in the PITY BUCKET! I am soaking up the REALITIES of life. Believe me, it isn't pretty!

LaVida, 39, cashier Not listening to every single word my parents ever told me! My life ended up totally screwed up because I did the exact opposite of what they told me not to! Because of this, I had a baby at sixteen. I have been battling drug addiction [and] spousal abuse for the past twenty-two years and thought I would NEVER see the day that I got off of probation! It was a long, hard road with many bumps along the way, but I overcame it all . . . finally!

But the fact still remains: had I taken my parents' advice way back when, I would have spared myself all the needless pain I went through, both mentally and physically!

Thanks for letting me get that out. Sometimes it's hard to admit it to other people, especially your parents. They just say, "I told you so."

Kimberly, 31, proud mom/devoted wife Although I am young in years, my life experiences add years of both knowledge and regrets. As a survivor of unspeakable emotional abuse at home, I continued in the tradition and married a monster at the age of nineteen. For nine years I lived in silence, believing my secret was safe and accepting the beatings as if I had earned them.

That is not my biggest regret, but the following is: one day, after returning home from the grocery store with my two young sons (ages three and four at the time), I took the beating I'm lucky to have survived. I don't remember how I got to the emergency room, but as I lay there on the cold, hard gurney I overheard my four-year-old son explaining to the doctor that "mommy had an accident; she falls down all the time. Hurry up and fix her, or my little brother will have an accident, too," his brave voice obviously masking his concern for his brother who was alone with dad.

At that moment, I opened my eyes and saw that little man, following his mommy's example, believing with all of his heart that what he was doing was right. As my vision cleared, I saw that his little face was covered with a bandage, and his tear-stained face fought to remain composed. Alarmed, I sat straight up and carefully chose the words as I asked the doctor how serious his injury was. The doctor peeled back the bandage to reveal twenty-three fresh stitches surrounded by a bruise that nearly covered his entire right cheek. Without saying a word, the doctor let me know that he knew what had really happened; his eyes burned mine with anger and pity.

To make a long story short, I didn't leave "the monster" that day or the next. Two years later I took my boys and ran for dear life, something I should've done long ago. But to this day, my son remembers that day in the emergency room, and the events that led up to that day. I had taken longer than "the monster" thought I should have. I should've been no longer than thirty minutes; I was gone for forty-five. I turned my back as he yelled at me. I never saw it coming, nor did I see my brave little boy jump in the way of the blow.

When a grown man's fist with all of that rage-driven strength connects with the tender skin of a child, the result is horrific. I don't remember how I lost consciousness—I'm glad I don't—but I will forever remember that little boy's eyes pleading with me to end it all and run away. I couldn't look in his eyes; the guilt was overwhelming. For two more years he witnessed the beatings, but never again tried to defend me like he had that day. I assumed the reason to be that of self-preservation, but how wrong I was.

"Mommy, I'm little, and dad is so big. I will get beat up bad if you don't help me." My biggest regret lies there. I was so distracted by the lifestyle I was used to, that I didn't even real-ize what my brave little boy had said. There were people all around that could help me—they outnumber "the monster" by far—but no one ever made me feel as strong as my son did that day. Although I hadn't taught him by example that what his father did was wrong, my son's simple words lifted me above the haze long enough to see the possibilities that lie ahead for the three of us, if I would just do what we both knew to be right.

Today we are fine, happy and whole. I married the man I'm sure was made just for me. My boys, me, and our new baby girl don't look back anymore, but every once in a while I think back and remember the four-year-old boy that saved us all, and marvel at the amazing person he is today.

chapter 8

The Lighter Side

Variety's the very spice of life.

—William Cowper

Regrets, by their nature, tend to deal with rather weighty subjects. However, the majority of submissions to RegretsOnly.com weren't dispiriting at all. In fact, whether intentional or not, many were quite amusing.

These are the "lightest" regrets of the bunch: light in tone, yet heavy on variety. Out of all the regrets that comprise this section, none fit easily into one category or another. Some are weird; others are wacky, yet all are distinct in their own way.

People sent various quips, quotes, anecdotes, and observations. One local church even mailed me a videotape. On the cover is a color photo of the cosmos. You know the picture: spiraling, celestial gases and dust encircled by, as the late

Carl Sagan would say, "billions and billions" of stars. Printed above this galaxy—in white, capital letters—is, "THE ULTIMATE QUESTION." The copy goes on to say:

Life presents us with many questions. These questions range from the trivial to the very important. However, there is really only one question that deserves to be called "The Ultimate Question."

I still haven't opened the tape. I just pray they consider my question—What is your biggest regret in life?—to be "important" rather than "trivial." (For some reason, though, something tells me they really don't consider my question to be "THE ULTIMATE QUESTION.")

But regardless of the questions being asked, I was always glad to hear from people who, no matter what, still retain their sense of humor. Especially the British: you gotta love 'em.

◆ ◆ ◆

Andy, 30, finance analyst My greatest regret in life is buying the *Graceland* album by Paul Simon. It put me off South African music for a long time.

Dawn, 37, copywriter I regret not liking the taste of butter. I'm not a fussy eater; I like everything. I'll try anything new, whatever. So imagine how frustrating it is to not like the taste of butter.

A business meeting with sandwiches or filled rolls, I can't eat anything because more than likely, there'll be butter. Even if they're not, I can hardly find out by dissecting the sandwich in front of everyone. When I don't eat, someone always comments and I find myself explaining that I don't like the taste of butter. Then I see that I've given the impression I'm fussy, awkward, a problem.

Take an Italian restaurant: Let's all order garlic bread. I love garlic and bread, but I can't stand the taste of the butter used to cook it. Suddenly, I'm the pooper because I'm not eating the garlic bread. Visiting friends for tea, scones are always dolloped with butter. In fact, the greater the host shows hospitality, the more butter that's on the scone. I love scones; I just can't stand the taste of butter, but I look rude if I scrape off the butter.

Eventually, when I was old enough to realise that I could tell people I can't stand the taste of butter, I started to spread the word. But no one remembers. My own father still passes me the butter if we breakfast together.

Why doesn't anyone remember? Every day, I regret that I can't stand the taste of butter.

Ted, 59, retired I retired last fall; that is not what I regret. What I regret is moving to Miami, Florida. Miami is pure hell on Earth.

Name withheld, 23, homemaker This may seem petty; I have too many regrets than I would like to admit. The one I am battling right now is an idiotic auto purchase I made for a used car with 66,000 miles on it opposed to a brand new one. What was I thinking?

Krystal, 10, child/student I regret eating cigarettes when I was five. They made me sick.

Scott, 10, school I wish that I was a cobbler's child. I like to play outside in bare feet. It feels good to feel the grass and even the sidewalk on your bare feet. It makes my mom freak out. She thinks I could cut my feet, but it has never happened. My dad is cool with it; says he played in bare feet a lot when he was a kid, too, and if he were a cobbler that I would have to go barefoot. Thanks for listening to me.

Pedro, 29, dentist When I was in high school I never put forth the effort to meet any girls. Now I'm a twenty-nine-year-old virgin. I have no dignity or pride. I don't think I'm ever going to get laid. Can someone please help me? If you meet a guy named Pedro and you think it might be me, please help me out, male or female.

Terri, 40, caterer I regret not having an apartment of my own. I went from my parents' home to my husband's home. I just want to know if I'm clean or messy.

Heather, 27, ballerina I regret accepting a job at a nonprofit because it means I make NO money.

Tom, 48, dentist For a time, I lived across the street from a nice family who had a yellow lab. Actually, he was almost white. He was very nice; the whole neighborhood liked him. He liked me because I sometimes had doggie treats in my pockets. He started greeting me with a song and I started answering back, imitating his ululation. Together, we made a horrible duet. I regret that I did not sing more with Smokey.

Name withheld, 47, housewife/mother I regret I didn't overcome my abnormal fear of dentists. I regret that I avoided the dentists at all cost. I regret my earliest experiences of that hated dentist. I regret that I didn't know the facts about the deadly toxin, fluoride, and that I had dutifully taken the fluoride pills given to my mother by the mean, rotten dentist she forced me to go to. I regret that my teeth crumbled considerably after the birth of my child. I regret that we never had the money to get even a small amount of dentistry done due to money and fears. I regret that only now do we have insurance to cover dental when I am forty-seven and could very well be at the end of a healthy cycle of living, making the expense of new dentures or bridges very expensive, indeed.

I mean, I could go through the dentist overcoming my fears; get some fake teeth or caps or bridges or dentures, only to get sick and drop dead within a decade and the teeth still, more or less new, and I would regret that, too.

Fred, 56, retired/part-time database designer I think my biggest regret is that women aren't really in political power. I think there would be much less bloodshed than we see today if they were. I also regret the power that individuals like presidents have. If my wishes were to come true, we would have a safer world, but at the expense of the economies of the dominants. No bad thing!

Judi, 56, computers I regret that I could not be a white male at any time. It would have helped me in my career.

Diana, 45, professional organizer Fear. FEAR. F-E-A-R. I regret that I have allowed unfounded, made-up-in-my-own-imagination FEAR stop me from doing the things I want to do because, as I get older and more experienced, I realize that FEAR is nothing more than a false reality that I create myself.

I have learned that everyone else is just as FEARFUL as I

am. But if I reach out to another fearful person during MY OWN FEAR, then it helps BOTH of us be FEARLESS. Fear is nothing but an excuse to resist *Carpe Momento* (Seize the moment!).

Why do I resist *Carpe Momento*? Why else? I'm SCARED!

Petra, 23, student I regret many things in my life: rude things I said when I shouldn't be rude; not saying rude things when I should. But what I regret most is the fact that I cannot forget them. I have a very good memory anyway and, of course, it can be handy; only it is extremely tiring that I still remember the boasting I did as four-year-old child. I don't hold myself responsible, but I regret the fact that I was lying. I still remember that I tried to fight once, and I couldn't win. No matter that the fight wasn't fair, I should have won or never picked that fight. I still remember—and regret.

Name withheld, 56, service I am proud to be born in a country of Mahatma Gandhi, but regret being ruled by Mafia-type politicians.

Name withheld, 41, telecommunications engineer I regret being born in this country [Indonesia] with the bloody, slicky [*sic*] policy. We are in the year of living dangerously, where "bad people" can easily control your life. If I have the second chance, I would rather be living or been born in Canada or U.S., where the LAW is blind. In my country, the

LAW is Money and Power. But I didn't hate the people, except the policy created by the new order government.

I have been cheated by the government since I was born, where ethics became strong differences in having my rights. During [these] forty-one years, my family and I became victim[s] of anything, from the way you get your ID [to] your chance to school. . . .

I want my children to have the chance to live in a real democracy country.

Russell, 46, scientist I regret that I believed various people, in various positions of authority, at various times in my life, actually had my best interests in mind when they "promised" me something. Always get it in writing.

Garry, 47, facilities engineering manager I regret "missing" the free love of the '60s. I currently live in the San Francisco area, but grew up in the Midwest.

Roberta, 45, ad agency owner When I was seventeen, I had a Wiccan friend of mine prepare a love spell for the young man I was dating. But I was warned I had to be with him on a certain date, within a certain time. I did the incantations as instructed, but as luck would have it, my folks grounded me and I couldn't see him when we were supposed to get together.

I called and told him, and he said, "No problem. We'll get together the next day."

Next day he calls me and sounds "funny." First, he's telling me how much he genuinely likes me and enjoys my company. Then he says he can't see me anymore because he met someone the day before and he's totally in love.

Whoa. Am I sorry. This was almost thirty years ago, so I hope the spell faded of its own accord. Ron, if you're out there, I'm really, really sorry for trying to screw with your head. And oh, I NEVER, EVER did magic again.

Name withheld, 41, student I am a new computer owner and user. I am still learning a lot about computers. I signed on to a Web site for a thirty-day trial for $39.95—unwittingly—thinking I was signing on for a three-day trial for $1.95. There was no way to cancel it.

I spent hours the next day, until I finally found an 800 number to call and cancel. Unfortunately, I'm stuck with the $39.95. What a rip-off! It's not even worth it! You live and learn. Watch out for scams and be careful what you sign up for. It could have been a lot worse, I guess.

Mike, 25, engineer I regret wasting so much time surfing the Internet. I could have been doing something useful with my time.

Seamus, 36, banking analyst I'm sorry that the Web came into existence as it gives sad people the opportunity to express themselves anonymously, when they'd be better off in the bar, getting it off their chest.

Jon, 46, retail manager The regret quotation that I recommend to you comes from [Robert] Heinlein's *Stranger in a Strange Land.* The old man says, "The only thing I regret are the temptations I resisted."

John, 69, sound designer I only want to call your attention to Bertrand Russell's Noble Prize acceptance speech. In it, he cites an Italian nobleman who was asked on his deathbed by the priest if he had any regrets.

"Yes," he replied. "I once entertained the Pope and the Emperor simultaneously and I took them to my tower to show them the view. I have always regretted that I neglected to push them both off, which would have given me immortal fame."

History fails to relate whether the priest granted him absolution.

chapter 9

I've Got to Be Me

This above all: to thine own self be true,
And it must follow, as the night the day,
Thou canst not then be false to any man.

—William Shakespeare, *Hamlet*, act I

Assertiveness, independence, and personal growth coalesce into what is perhaps the most philosophical section of all. Here, self-discovery is the name of the game, with sexuality as the dominant theme.

It's about people being truly comfortable with their identity. That means coming to terms with who they are versus what society expects them to be. While some do, indeed, find their true spirit, others still hand-carry their emotional baggage.

Of course, there's also a flip side—the people who don't

beat themselves up over the choices they've made. They simply refuse to dwell on the past. They either have few regrets or none whatsoever. Their motto: learn from your mistakes and move on.

What impressed me most about *all* these respondents was the incredible depth of thinking by young and old alike. Regrets become their springboard to expound on a host of other topics—the kind of topics we never discussed in overcrowded college classes.

The scene was UCLA where I attended my first—and only—philosophy class taught by a visiting professor from UC Irvine. He was a nice enough guy, but there was one problem: he had a *severe* and persistent stutter.

Three times a week, his interminable lectures featured renowned philosophy mavens such as Sartre, Kierkegaard, Hegel, and Kant. (Over the entire course I kept thinking, "Help me! I just KANT understand this stuff!")

To me, it was nothing but convoluted, highbrow nonsense that had no relevance or meaning to real life. Needless to say, I was miserably lost for most of the term and ended up with a C.

Yes, I regret taking his class. That's why, after more than twenty years, it's so refreshing to see reasoned thinking from many modern day "philosophers."

In other words, from people who actually make sense.

◆ ◆ ◆

Jane, 33, administrative The question is, "Should I be regretful about anything?" After all, isn't the main purpose of our existence for our souls to collect learning experiences in each lifetime? No matter how awful or wonderful? Every choice we make, every person we meet, everything we do—and the way we decide to react to it all—helps to shape who we are.

I must say, in thirty-three years, I truly have a lot more life experience than I care to have. Sadly, for some of us, life has to be extra hard, extra cruel, in order for us to learn lessons. Then there are others whose lives seem to "coast by" with such ease; so little care in the world—and very little struggle.

I am almost ashamed to say I envy them sometimes. But I know, without my experiences, I wouldn't be the person I am. I can't regret that.

I came into the world as a multiracial individual during a time when society recognized only a circle or square, and here I am— an octagon. No matter where you go, what you do, you never quite "fit in." Things have changed [and] progressed, but not enough so I can have a place; can find acceptance. I regret that.

Abandoned, then kidnapped as a child; abused, then neglected throughout my formative years; shunned and persecuted by my peers, it made me so withdrawn. I still am most of the time.

"What doesn't break you, makes you stronger" and *"God only gives you as much as you can handle."* If that's true, then I don't regret my ability to persevere. I cannot regret being a C

student when I was honor-roll material. I can still hear my mother's words: "It doesn't matter what your grades are, only that you finish school." I graduated at sixteen, came in contact with my first computer, and found my calling.

I was date-raped for my first sexual experience, had my first child by twenty [and] two failed marriages; now, a single parent of three kids with three different fathers. Not what I was looking for. But as I look into my children's faces and see the exceptional human beings I am having the honor to raise and bring into the world, how can I regret that?

My life has been far from easy. My children will be grown in ten years; I'm going to live to see 100. With all the concerns and fears I may have, my Quality of Life continues to improve with age.

And I certainly don't regret that.

Jamie, 20, customer service When I was going to high school, I kissed my girlfriend before class. I regret doing that. As soon as it happened, my life was no longer the same. I was no longer invisible to all my classmates. I was naked and they took advantage of that.

My lunch periods were interrupted every day with hundreds of kids asking about it. I wouldn't advise coming out in school. I was ridiculed at gym, ridiculed by the principal, ridiculed by people whom I thought were friends. Got thrown into lockers [and] punched walking down the hallway.

No longer invisible.

Kyra, 48, office administration For the most part, I have no regrets. I firmly believe that everything happens for a reason, and everything that happens to us is a necessary step to get us where we need to go. Had I taken a different path, I would not be where I am today, good or bad. I may not have met my ex-husband, which led to becoming mother to my beloved daughter. Although my marriage ended, I have never regretted marrying this man and still think very highly of him. We consider each other friends, as well as parents to our daughter.

Having said all that, to be honest, I must say that I regret that I never called my mother's bluff.

Let me explain: As a teenager and young adult (I suppose even as a child, though I don't remember), every time I tried to make a real decision for myself, I was told I would be "disowned" if I proceeded with whatever plan I had. Sometimes I was even threatened with being disowned for things that had never occurred to me.

Once, as a teen, I was told that if I dated an Asian or a black man, I would be disowned. I hadn't even thought about it one way or the other. Later, having won a state scholarship grant, I wanted to go away to school. My wishes met with threats of being disowned.

In 1971, when I was nineteen, my best friend from college (I commuted to school while living at home) was going to buy a house and wanted me as one of five roommates. This was my buddy: a young man, well known to the entire family, but not the least interested in me romantically. When I told my mother that I wanted to move out and into Jim's house (having the entire basement apartment all to myself), I was again threatened with being disowned. She said no daughter of hers was going to live with a man.

This continued on, even after I had moved out (at twenty-one, after a horrible confrontation and being called terrible names by my mother), and even a bit after I was married. I loved my mother and father dearly and the idea of being disowned scared me senseless, even though I really didn't know what that would mean, if anything.

Finally, when my mother was in her late seventies or early eighties, she told me that she had been date-raped twice as a young woman. The proverbial lightbulb went on over my head, as I finally understood her motivations: she thought that by keeping an inordinately tight rein on me—even using threats, if necessary—she could protect me and calm her own mind.

I only wonder what would have happened if I had been allowed to make decisions, right or wrong, and learn from them. I think I wouldn't have the self-doubts that still sometimes plague me, nor would I have fears of being left "high and dry."

In my mother's defense, I must say that she also gave me the incredible strengths that I have, and the strong faith and belief in God. She did a lot right. I am so happy that, as a mother, I have been able to recognize the good, throw out the bad, and be much more the kind of parent I had wished for as a child.

I learned to respect my daughter's autonomy and individuality, while still requiring her to take responsibility for her actions. In a way, I parented myself while parenting my daughter. Through necessity, as a single parent and fending for the two of us, I grew up very suddenly—*finally*—in my thirties. I only wish I had learned how to be a grown-up while actually getting there.

Diana, 53, technical/administrative support I regret that I have allowed anger and stubbornness to govern my responses and actions in life, to the point that they have shaped my persona and destiny as surely as if I had plotted it all on a grid.

I suppose that the circumstances of birth (congenital deformations of my legs) had a great deal to do with that anger and stubbornness. After all, to get anywhere in this world, you need to use both just to keep your head above water—even if you are whole. However, at some point, those possible qualities became submerged and the negative side intensified to the point that I almost ruined my daughters' lives, too. Thankfully, they are a product of more than just my manipulation.

The anger is still there, the stubbornness is still there, but I have allowed honesty to rise and help free me from the powerful negative effects. It didn't happen in my youth; it didn't happen in my middle years, but has evolved to become more important than the anger.

Mostly, I regret that the sum of my life has not been of more benefit to the whole. Instead of grasping the problems and working them out, I stubbornly cling to them and allow them to rule. It is difficult dealing with the "could have beens" or "want to be" when you are frozen in place by the dark forebodings evoked by anger and brooding. Nonproductive as they may be, there has been a learning process throughout that may, someday, allow me to contribute rather than worry.

It has happened occasionally; it may happen again.

Albin, 51, performer In 1966, at the age of nineteen, I "came out" to my parents. At that time, even the phrase "coming out" wasn't used and homosexuality was something never discussed in my provincial little community. Before I knew what was happening, my parents whisked me to see our doctor who immediately made an appointment for me to see a psychiatrist.

During the course of the weeks leading up to my appointment, I felt very confused and sad. I knew I wasn't mad—just different from all the people I knew. I felt I was the only one to be troubled in this way; knew no other gay people and knew of nowhere and nobody to whom I could turn for help and advice. So I cancelled my appointment with the psychiatrist, told my parents that it had been a "phase I was going through" and that I was "better now."

Eventually, under peer and family pressure, I married and managed to father two wonderful daughters and remained married and faithful for seventeen years. Then, one June night, my wife said, "I'll have to tell you this or my headache will never go." She told me she was a lesbian and had been all her life. She said she was in the middle of an affair the day we married, and had had numerous affairs since.

She had fallen in love with a girl at work, she said, and was leaving me. Twenty-five minutes later, she was gone. We had to wake the children up to tell them.

How ironic! After being married for seventeen years, with neither of us aware of each other's sexuality, she, bless her (and I mean that), left to follow her true sexual calling, leaving me (also homosexual) to continue hiding my sexuality for professional and family reasons. It also seems to me ironic that she had had a number of affairs over the years, but I had remained largely faithful, yet frustrated.

This all confused my two girls who, ages twelve and thirteen, doubted their own sexuality for a time.

I was in a responsible and fairly public, high-profile position, so [I] carried on working and bringing up my two daughters to the best of my ability. I remember my younger daughter taking my hand one time and saying, "Don't you 'turn,' Dad. I couldn't cope with two in the family. . . . "

My girls have both left home and are leading fulfilled and happy lives—and I am blessed with two grandchildren.

Now I'm over fifty, and although I have had occasional partners, age and health have conspired to make the chances of real fulfillment and happiness something only to be dreamed of. To compensate, I lead a full, hectic life, soaking myself in performances of all kinds: plays, musicals, storytelling, readings, directing—even a little performing as a drag artist. So I am reasonably content and have much to be thankful for: friends to whom I am "out" and love me; family to whom I am NOT "out" and love me.

I suppose my one regret is that I didn't stand firm at the age of nineteen and fight my corner. But it was difficult then. And, I suppose, in many ways it still is for young men and women to publicly acknowledge their sexuality.

Oh, there we are! Not a world shattering regret and one that I can live with, but a regret all the same.

Steve, 42, accountant I've known my only real regret in life for a long time now: I always regretted not telling my mother that I was gay before she died. The rest of my family and I are estranged, in large part (I think) due to my "sinful" lifestyle. I think my mother, though, would have embraced me, regardless. I always imagined that she'd even go out drinking at gay bars with me.

Charlotte, 23, teacher When I was fifteen, I met an older girl in art class who was very, very sophisticated and very, very beautiful. We became friends, and one night during winter break, she asked me to spend the night. We drank some beers, watched TV, and both tired out about two in the morning.

We crawled in bed and snuggled up against each other, and she asked if I thought she was cute. I told her I thought she was very pretty and she told me I was "hot." She put her hand on·my breast, but I pretended I was asleep so I wouldn't have to respond. I did have sexual feelings for her, but I didn't know how to express them. We were never as close after that and eventually grew apart.

I last saw her before she left for college a few years ago and she gave me a hug. Last I heard, she had gotten married to a football player; I'm engaged to a jazz singer now.

I never slept with a girl and I probably never will. I wish I had done it with her. What was I afraid of?

Chuck, 62, retired teacher I was born at a time when I didn't even know there was such a thing as "gay," but knew something was wrong. Later, when I understood, fear and self-hatred kept me miserable my whole life and ruined me emotionally. Now out, and intellectually at peace, I still suffer from a huge amount of "baggage." Latest research shows stress-induced depression causes permanent physical brain damage. I have it.

Anyone out there who is gay, or who is trying to force people to stay in the closet or "change," listen up: It is abuse to make people ashamed of the way they are. Psychological abuse is in many ways worse than physical abuse.

Anyone who says, "I hate the sin, but love the sinner" is a liar. The so-called "sin" is part of the person—and celibacy is not a humane option, believe me.

Eric, 54, senior manager/shipping industry My biggest regret is that I allowed society and my family to push me deep into denial in my teenage years regarding my homosexuality. As a result, I wasted at least ten years of my life—probably more—trying to "cure" myself. In doing so, I hurt the woman I married, my family, and nearly drove myself crazy. When I finally did accept that I was gay and there was no way to change it, I did come out. Of course, I ruined my marriage and, because of the trauma it caused me, I did some things that really hurt my family and others close to me.

Looking back at those times nearly twenty-five years ago, it still makes me extremely unhappy that a large part of our society discriminates against homosexuals. More young people will have to endure the same hardships I did. Fortunately, many people have realized that homosexuality is normal, and times are not nearly as difficult now as they were in the 1950s and 1960s.

I am truly comfortable with my sexual orientation. I've been in a loving and committed relationship for over seventeen years. I am a business and civic leader in my community, and I find that most people accept me as I am. I have found that, by the time many of my associates find out that I have a partner of the same sex, I have earned their respect through hard work, maintenance of high standards, and reliability. When they learn that I am gay it is fairly difficult for them to ignore all the other factors that allowed me to win their trust and friendship in the first place.

My only hope is that I can make life easier for those who come after me.

Thomas, 20, emergency medical technician I only regret that I had sometimes fallen in love with the wrong people. Some of my relationships were one-sided or were a total disaster. I also regret that I waited too long to discover myself; the person that I really am, instead of trying to be what everyone else wanted me to be.

I regret that I did not tell my parents about the person I really was: I did not tell them that I liked guys just as much as I liked girls. I regret not telling them about all the different kinds of relationships I had with guys my age, and girls, as well. I regret that I had to hide my "bi" side from everyone.

Tara, 38, administrative assistant My biggest regret is having a sex change operation [and] putting the ones I loved so dearly through all the problems and issues that I did, especially my parents. After considering all I put them through and all I put myself through, it now just doesn't seem worth it. I have come full circle in the realization that no matter how far you run away, you can never hide from your true self.

I spent many years in therapy and counseling trying to find my so-called self—changing myself to a person I thought I wanted to be, taking hormones and having operations that would alter my body and my mind to a degree. I feel no less and no more happier than before; I'm just in a different state of being.

I'm judged differently, and because of my gender change, I am accepted into a different role now [as] a woman. However, all I thought would make me free and content, I've found that there are as many problems, worries, and headaches being a woman as there are a male—it's just a different type.

I feel, after all was said and done, I could have learned to be as happy and content staying the way I was without bringing so much worry and heartache to the ones I loved.

Michelle, 35, market analyst All of my life, from the time I was twelve or so, I can remember saying to myself, "Why have regret?" Anything can be resolved or undone or recaptured at another time in our lives. At thirty-five, I am beginning to see that there will be one thing in my life that I cannot recapture or undo or resolve if I wait too much longer.

I am a thirty-five-year-old woman who has never been lucky enough to meet someone and have a family. I know that if I do not have a child before I am forty, that the regret will consume me. Knowing this with absolute certainty, I have decided to have a child without waiting for "Mr. Right."

Liz, 44, Web/graphic designer While I don't regret having my two wonderful sons, there are things that I do regret. I guess that the major regret in my life was keeping my true feelings inside of myself for the past eighteen years. For the love of my children, I lost my identity and pasted myself as a quiet mouse of a mother and housewife, finding that, when I had a thought that went against that of my husband, it was better for myself and the children not to voice my feelings.

I regret not having what I needed to step forward and go against ideas that I knew took my self-esteem away—leaving me with not much more than what I was given. I regret having to bite my tongue when I didn't agree. I regret believing what I was told by my husband and his religion about the place of women as being the "right way." I regret that I'm still trapped within the past eighteen years.

On the better side, I am working to pull myself out of my past and become my own person, once more. Then again, I may regret that I'm still full of fear.

Garry, 39, IT manager My regret is an almost personal belief. When I was small, I was constantly told that I was shy. As a result, I came to believe this about myself and never pushed my way forward, never asked that girl out, never went for the big job, lacked any sort of confidence.

I have brains and I'm told a modicum of looks, a wife and daughter, and now, a decent, well-paid job. But my regret is that everything took so long to get started. It wasn't until I had turned thirty that I felt I started to blossom as a person. If I could have only known the positives about myself at the age of fifteen or twenty, things would have been so different.

Name withheld, 23, student I regret not correcting my friend. My friend started to call me the "Master Manipulator" a few years back because he felt that I coerced my friends into following whatever I wanted to do. Although I am very free with my opinion and like to state my case, I would never try to control my friends in any way. But regardless, I didn't think the saying would cause any harm and I must admit, it boosted my ego a bit to think that I had that much control.

Now, a couple years later, that phrase has sunk in more than I could have ever imagined. When I say anything, I can see it in my friends' eyes how some of them don't trust me anymore. I have only lied to them once (about liking a girl; not a big offense) yet now, I have a stigma attached, be it said or unsaid. It has ended up killing one friendship and severely hampering two others. All of these friendships were very dear to me and I hate to lose any. I regret being so dumb and letting this phrase wreck my reputation.

One other note: I read another regret [on your Web site] from a seventh-grader that said, "I regret that I hesitate when I talk when I am trying to talk to girls." It amazes me how some regrets can be applied to any age.

Francesca, 34, Spanish professor I am the youngest of eight children and have benefited greatly from my mother's advice. [She] has been the only person I've ever really listened to. Despite my initial protestations, she convinced me to go to college, which blossomed into a year abroad in Germany where I ended up in Spain as a language teacher and musician.

I eventually returned to the U.S. to pursue my Ph.D. in Literature in a program that was both stimulating and intimidating for me. During these intellectual pursuits, I regret not listening to much of the sage advice that was generously offered by professors and nonprofessionals alike. Many people have tried to mentor me over the years; I am independent to a fault and have hoarded all my potential within the tight confines of lone projects and endeavors. This has paid off well, as I am a confident, committed professor.

But I feel that I have reached only a shred of my potential to communicate my ideas and to reach out to others. I regret not listening to other people's suggestions, which were always a generous offer to polish my rough surface. Life would have been a lot easier.

Name withheld, 49, retired At an early age, I found a way to live without regrets. An ailing, eighty-nine-year-old lady said to me, "You will never regret the things you do in this life; only the things you did *not* do." She was in a care home, dying of cancer, and I was a volunteer there, at age fifteen. She impressed me, and I began to live my life to the fullest. Five months later, she died.

I have worked smart—not hard—in my lifetime, and retired at thirty-five always doing what I do best: that is, living my life to the fullest. Doing for others is how I spend a lot of my time, building a life without regrets.

Gordon, 61, retired At age sixty-one, looking back, I find the question should not be what you regret, but how well you lived your life. You should not regret perceived missed opportunities, but look at all the experiences and knowledge you have enjoyed. Hindsight is not a good measure of what your life is about; you just learn from it and live a better life.

Make a list of five things that you will allow to bother you, and make all the rest not worth the energy to fret about. You will find that, after a time, you won't be able to remember the five things that bothered you. My take is that you should live your life doing as little damage as possible to the Earth and life and people that live on it.

John, 45, fire captain Been working as a firefighter for twenty-one years; now a captain in a metropolitan fire department. Absolutely no regrets—though there is that one particular warehouse fire where I should have ducked at the right time, and saved myself a trip to the hospital.

Ann, 57, retired I wouldn't change one thing of my life. I have made mistakes, but that was how I was to learn. I am totally happy with myself and life. I do wish I could influence people to feel the same way I do, and have the joy and love that I have had and seem to continue to have.

I have no regrets because I believe that our lives are supposed to be good and bad. We are here to learn from our experiences, we hope. Because my spiritual life is so awesome, I am completely happy. My only regret is that I didn't learn this long before now. But if I were supposed to learn earlier, I would have.

I do regret the way the world is, but feel if we pray and think positive and listen to the messages that are coming to us through books, TV, etc., we can do something about it.

Everyone can tell about the regrets or guilt, but how many are asked to look at the good in their lives? My biggest regret now is that so many churches teach fear because they want control. Therefore, you have people "regretting" or feeling guilty when they shouldn't.

Leon, 43, teacher I regret nothing. Regrets without action are futile. You cannot reconstruct the past, but you can learn from your mistakes. Regret involves the process of dwelling on the past in a negative and unconstructive fashion.

Apologies, atonement, service to negate what you might have done or whom you might have slighted, would be more effective if they were the natural result of regret. But to dwell on the past in a way that is a kind of solipsistic emotional wallowing that helps no one—least of all the person who makes the regrets—is to be condemned. It only "sanctifies" the actions in a form of imagined self-reflection, with no pragmatic outcome.

The act of regretting is an idle sop to conscience and would better be put aside for mawkish sentimentality. It is the emotional equivalent of the "Lassie film" if action to improve is not part of the process of regret.

Adam, 25, student I have long had a policy on regret: don't have any. There have been many things in my life which caused me pain and sorrow, and many that have brought me joy. But to change those things that had caused me pain would be to alter the timeline of my life. Without the bad times, who knows if I would have experienced the good times?

It's like chaos theory: a butterfly flaps its wings in China, and through an intricate series of interconnected events, you get a tornado in Oklahoma. Change one step along the way, and maybe you get snow in Colorado.

The same is true for life: change one step along the way and you wind up with an entirely different outcome.

Terry, 33, architecture At times I think that I have regrets, however, I often later realize that I should not have regrets about many (maybe even all) of the instances that I would possibly have considered a regret. I have very clearly come to see, just in this past year, how the many aspects of our lives shape us into who we are. Without the events that we may, for a period of time, consider regrets, we might never accomplish what we are meant to accomplish (or what we set out to accomplish).

It is truly amazing when you can look at your "best accomplishments" and realize their insignificance, and look at your "deepest regrets" and realize their great value!

Stephanie, 31, (no occupation given) I was diagnosed with an illness three years ago that totally disrupted my life. Because of this illness, and the subsequent treatments I've undergone due to it, many changes have occurred in my life that have caused me to reexamine what I value; what I've done with my life up to this point; and what is really important to me in terms of other people and myself.

Before I was diagnosed, I thought my life was a hell. I didn't have enough money. I couldn't buy this or that. I didn't get along with my parents. I didn't have a brand new car and most of my friends did, etc., etc. Now, after becoming ill, I am unable to work. I feel sick and experience pain almost every day. Small things are very hard for me to do now. I cannot have children. All of these elements, plus others, have caused a deep depression that has been very difficult to overcome.

Now, I look back at what I considered my "difficult and bleak" life of only a few years ago. I realize now, how much I truly did have back then, and of all the opportunities I missed because I felt bitter and angry, or I thought I had so much time to "do them later." I realize now, how special it was just being able to take myself for a car ride, or being able to go to a movie with my friends. I realize now, that I SHOULD HAVE taken the various opportunities I was presented with back then to meet new friends, further my education, [and] just appreciate what I had and be happy with it all.

I regret not doing more, appreciating the world more, and appreciating how lucky I really was. I let superficial and material wants (and the resulting bitterness and anger from those wants) color my life to the point of not letting me truly live life the way I should have. I was an immature person back then, in many ways, and I wish I could take back all the years I wasted giving in to my manufactured "angst," when in reality, I really did have a very blessed life in terms of my health and possible potential.

The one result of my illness that I am grateful for is a new perspective on life, and what is truly special and priceless. I hope I will never lose that new angle on life. Being sick, and unable to do the things I want, has taught me how valuable the little things are in life—things you can't buy—and how unimportant all the superficial garbage is; and how, if you let it, that superficial/materialistic fixation only takes away from a person more than it adds to a life.

I am going to try, from now on, to not look back at my life and think of all the time I wasted bemoaning what I don't have and instead, realize how lucky I am to have the things I do.

chapter 10

Etched Forever

You ain't heard nothin' yet, folks.

—Al Jolson in *The Jazz Singer,* 1927

Surely, you've found at least one or two memorable regrets among the group. Written by people you never thought you'd relate to, yet there they are: people like you, whose unforgettable stories will stay with you a while.

The stories selected for this chapter were chosen not because they were the most eloquent or even the most inspirational, but I chose them for three other reasons:

First, each person wrote passionately and sensitively on the broader issues that affect most of us: childhood, adolescence, education, career, materialism, sexuality, family, children, independence, and self-esteem. These are, to me, the major elements that define one's life.

Second, I was impressed by each person's point of view and by the vital questions a few of them raised. Quite frankly, if these people don't put things into perspective for you, nobody can.

Finally, the imagery associated with many of their regrets is seared into my brain, as if by a branding iron. No matter how much I try to forget them, I just can't. Because what they say shouldn't be forgotten.

So for me, these fourteen people and their moving stories will stick with me every single day—for the rest of my life.

♦ ♦ ♦

Carol, 38, medical transcriptionist I was raised in a very segregated and sheltered way: no watching "dirty TV" like *Candid Camera*; not being allowed to see news coverage of the Vietnam War; no interaction with people who weren't like my family (suburban/white/middle-class/Baptist). Hard work was almost a deity.

I was taught to say "Yes, ma'am" and "No, sir" and "Thank you, but no." I was taught to take whatever intimidation and mental/physical abuse was handed to me as though it were my favorite dish at the dinner table—processing it to ensure building a solid character.

Who I wanted to be was not who I was allowed to be. Presentation was everything and the façade of happiness and self-assuredness were necessary for the world to accept me.

I wanted someone to love me, fulfill me, need me, and put up with my feeble attempts of daring to be myself. I married the first person who could tolerate me. He loved me then and still does, now that I have moved on.

What I regret more than anything was failing to be myself before the age of thirty-five. I got pregnant when I was seventeen. Upon hearing the news, my then boyfriend's (later husband's) response was to pay for half the abortion. I didn't argue; I did what was expected of me. I should have asserted what I wanted. I should have been true to myself.

If I had been true to what I believed to be right rather than pleasing someone else, my life would have taken a much different path—perhaps one that had more to offer me in my later years, perhaps not, but certainly one that would have left me knowing what I find myself wondering now, at age thirty-eight:

Who am I?

Kayla, 20, student I regret painting my skin tan and highlighting my hair. I competed in a statewide beauty pageant. I made a conscious decision to be myself, but at the last minute I panicked and decided "myself" wasn't good enough. I placed in the Top 10 and I'm still proud of how I did, but I wish I recognized myself when I look at the pictures of my big day.

Nicole, 19, student I think the one thing that I really regret is having sex at a young age of fifteen. I honestly feel that when I started having sex I actually started having adult problems.

It hasn't been the same since.

I feel like I am entirely too young for my life. Taking on adult situations definitely puts a child in an adult's place, and I regret that. I regret that I missed my high school years trying to be what I am so tired of now. I hate being grown and I hate depending solely on me. I hate worrying about a love life; I wish I had never begun having a love life. It is impossible to try to be young at some things and a woman at others. My life is proof of this.

I have lived a double life all my life. I have secrets hidden within me that even *I* can't come to terms with, and in the end, I blame this all on sex.

I regret going too fast, I regret being "grown" and I regret that I even have a reason to regret.

Leigh, 28, unemployed/aspiring writer My biggest regret is leaving high school at seventeen. For a long time, I had a million other tiny regrets and I never thought that was one of them. Now, however, at twenty-eight, I've come to realize just how deeply that choice has affected my life.

I've been in and out of menial jobs for ten years. Although I had to leave school for medical reasons, my mother was disappointed. I'm not a stupid person; I'm quite well read and active in my local arts scene. I do volunteer work whenever I can. I also write stories and mentor the son of a friend. The reason I do all this is to make myself feel better about my dumb choice.

Recently, an old school chum approached me at a local bar and asked me if I would be attending our ten-year reunion. I had no idea what to tell him.

"Oh gee, don't you remember? I'm that moron who quit just before graduation!" That wouldn't sound too good.

It wasn't just that, though. I do have a high school diploma and did take a few college courses. But I just feel as though I missed out, you know? Missed hearing my name read out; missed seeing the look on my mom's face.

Now, I'm raising two young children and I grill them all the time about the importance of staying in school. Maybe that seems a bit superficial and strange, considering what I did.

But I want to sit in that auditorium eight years from now and watch my girl walk up to that podium.

I refuse to let my regret become hers as well.

Sheila, 43, teacher When I was seven, I was cycling downhill. I hit a metal fencepost at the bottom of the hill; I don't remember how or why. I was unconscious for about two hours and still cannot remember the accident.

I had a three-inch gash on my forehead and nose. It was sewn up as a temporary measure by a nurse. She told my father that it was very important that I return in six months to have it re-sewn neatly. She said that as I was so young, it would heal well.

When the day came for me to return to the hospital to have the plastic surgery, my mother would not take me. She said that my father (who was at work) did not want me to have it. The scar was wide, with obvious stitch marks. I said I was not going to go through life like that; I said I would walk down to the hospital on my own.

My regret is that I did not do it. Instead, I walked to school with my identical twin sister. I think now, that if I had started to walk toward the hospital, my mother would have given in and taken me there. As a result, I did not have the scar resewn until I was twenty. Therefore, it is still obvious.

I cannot believe I will have to go through life with this scar, especially as it would be almost invisible now if I had had the operation when I was seven. The scar is in such an obvious place: on my forehead and nose. The top of my nose is also slightly dented.

I am a teacher, so I am facing people all the time. It has definitely affected my confidence.

Craig, 40, factory worker The day I got out of high school I got a good paying summer job at a factory. My thoughts were to make the good money now, see the world and join the Navy or something, then maybe college. Just live life to the fullest, whether that meant ending up in a mansion in Beverly Hills or a grass hut on some tropical island.

Thing is, the summer job has now lasted twenty-two years. I never really saw the world and never went to anything higher than being the average, everyday guy. I settled in because of security and a decent paycheck.

But now, I have no stories to tell. Nothing but everyday stuff.

Vienne, 27, consultant My biggest regret in my twenty-seven years of existence is the fact that I never had enough courage to tell my mom what I've always wanted all these years. She always dictated how things should be—even in choosing my college degree. She wanted me to be SOMEONE, with a big name and impressive title. She wanted me to be a lawyer (like her) or a doctor, but I just couldn't see myself in those fields.

My interest was always in the arts, particularly in dance. I studied ballet and jazz and totally loved it. I never felt happier than those times when I was onstage dancing. But my mom couldn't see that. I wanted to continue dancing, but she always thought that dancing was just a hobby and not a real profession. I really wished she could have just been supportive. Since I wanted to please her and make her proud of me, I decided to put my dream aside and pursue a corporate career.

I took up my MBA, hoping that I would eventually forget about dancing and learn to like the prestige of wearing a powerful business suit to a top corporation every day. Now, at twenty-seven, I'm working as a consultant for an international management consulting company and earning quite well, but I'm not as happy as other people think I should be.

My love for dancing still haunts me. Every time I watch a dance concert, a movie, or musical with lots of dancing, tears start to form in my eyes. I always think, "That could have been me up there" or "That's the life I want." But I guess it's too late now.

At my age, it's obviously too late to build a career in dance. I've just decided to go back and take dance classes again, but I'll have to live knowing that dance for me will forever be just a hobby.

I guess I should have told my mom years ago what I really wanted. She could have been disappointed in me, but it's my life—and my happiness.

Name withheld, 52, private investigator I was born very smart. In high school, I was tested in the genius range and later qualified for MENSA. In the '70s, my younger sister got involved in the burgeoning computer industry and offered to help me learn about them and the possibilities available, as I was then contemplating a career change.

I applied my intellect to the issue and decided that the uses for computers would be very limited—and the profession a dead-end. A few years later, she bought into a new computer software company started by some geek in Washington and suggested that I do the same. I considered the option, and my intelligence helped me decide that Microsoft was definitely going to be a "flash in the pan"—with a very small market—so I declined.

Today, my semiretired sister and her husband left for their third vacation of this year. I'll most likely put in another seventy hours of work this week.

Sometimes, I regret being born so "smart."

Name withheld, 35, housewife In the short time I have been on the planet, I have lived several lifetimes. I regret that money cannot buy you happiness. It really can't. It can pay all your bills and make your wildest (material) dreams come true, but it destroys as much as it saves.

Some think they have it made when they hit the lottery; I see a few million or so new problems headed their way. Everything has its price.

Rich people are not nice; they are not pleasant to be around. The women are overly made up and bitchy. The men are crooks and wheeler-dealers. Everyone hits you up for "investment opportunities," no matter how large or small.

[People are] looking for a way to use you, and when you become no longer available to them, they dump you. Poof—no more phone calls, no more going out anywhere. Gone [are] old friends and new. I have bought people cars and lost their friendships. I have paid their bills just so they can run them up again. I regret that Man is a predictable beast.

We are no longer invited anywhere by our family because everything we have is nicer than what they have. We no longer associate with our old friends because we stopped making them "loans" or "gifts" of cash. We were paying them to play with us, so to speak. I regret this knowledge that when you have money, no one is truly your friend or interested in you as a person.

My thoughts, my feelings, my personality are of no consequence. It's all about what they can get out of me. My husband and I fight more than we did when we were "regular" people. I want to save and invest; he wants to give it away to every person with [his or her] hand out. We have discussed dividing the money 50/50. And to be absolutely honest, I don't want to wind up supporting him when his loser "friends" milk him dry of his last penny.

I find myself bored out of my mind. I have lavish, beautiful clothes; a new car; a brand-new house built to our specifications (what an education that was) and nowhere to go. My only solace is shopping for stuff I don't need or even want. I am invited to charity events, but the only reason I am invited is for my checkbook. If I had it to do over, I would never buy another lottery ticket as long as I live.

When I was one of the "working poor," I could have a discussion with someone and know they did not have any ulterior motives. When I was "regular people," I did not have the trappings of wealth, and therefore, I was no different than the next guy. I was not given special treatment. I was not put into a room by myself with one saleslady at my beck and call.

Hotels, airports, it's all the same: people with their fake smiles and platitudes. I regret that I don't have one single true friend in the world—not even the guy I am married to. I want for only one thing that I cannot buy: a friend. Someone to go to lunch with and talk about the headlines; what the neighbors are doing; someone to have out on the boat. Someone I go shopping with and not have to buy anything. Someone I don't have to pay for all the time. Someone who can pick up the tab once in a while. Is that too much to ask? Just a simple, honest, loyal friend.

I already have a dog. I got a large breed out of simple belligerence so it can eat those puffed up showpieces on sight. I purposely wear stained clothes around the house and sometimes out to the store, which really upsets our "class" of snobs.

I hate money. I hate being rich. I regret winning the six-million-dollar lottery. I very much regret winning the lottery.

Mollie, 76, retired Recently, I enjoyed the rare treat of having all three of my children with me at the same time. I took advantage of the opportunity to express my regret over having been too harsh in my discipline when they were growing up.

I was a single mother with three children and received no

support other than my two and sometimes three jobs. Because work demanded so much of my time, I was terrified of losing control of my family.

My son's response was, "Mom, none of us went to jail, did we?"

His two sisters applauded and said, "Here, here!" That relieved me of an emotional burden I'd borne for years.

Cindy, 43, mom/wife/professional volunteer It was November 1985. We were in JC Penney in Seattle, exchanging a tunic top for a black skirt. The holiday season was fast approaching as was evident by the sparkling decorations, the flurry of activity, and the anxious shoppers in the mall.

I was with my three-year-old son, Stevie. He had just recently been released from Swedish Hospital where he had undergone an experimental bone marrow transplant attempting to reverse his rare form of terminal leukemia. He was quite a sight in the stroller—knit cap covering his bald head; surgical mask over his nose and mouth protecting him from random germs. The stares he received from strangers set him on edge. Regardless, he was still a beautiful child.

My regret is born from the fact that as we approached the elevator inside Penney's, we had to pass the photo studio. There stood a long line of frazzled mothers—strollers in hand—filled with squirming children, dressed in their best clothes, waiting to have their holiday pictures taken.

I debated internally [about] asking loudly for all of their

attention and begging for their permission to take "cuts" by explaining our situation, and allowing us to go next and have Stevie photographed. However, I hesitated; I didn't want to publicly humiliate my son. His understanding of what was happening to him far exceeded his years.

I silently pushed his stroller to the elevator, shaking my head, not saying a word.

We returned to our apartment to learn the hospital had called. Stevie's blood counts were all off and he needed to be readmitted. We returned home to Michigan the following week: Stevie relapsed. Five days later, Stevie died.

Those photographs never taken would have been so precious—his last formal photographs. He was my first child; every step of his life had been documented in pictures.

To this day, I regret not having the courage to speak out and ask strangers for a moment of kindness, patience, and consideration for my child and ultimately, for me, what would have been a priceless treasure.

Danielle, 21, sales and marketing consultant I really didn't have to give this question too much thought. For the past three years I have struggled with my regret, endlessly. I am hoping this qualifies as a single regret and if not, I apologize. So here goes:

Ever since I was young—real young, about six or seven— everyone I came in contact with told me I was one of the most intelligent people they ever met. At seven, can you imagine?

I used to sit with my father at dinner and watch the evening news and at the end, he would turn off the TV, pick a topic, and ask me what I thought. For hours we would debate controversial issues like divorce, capital punishment, and separation of church and state. In school, I was enrolled in every enrichment program there was. I was actually invited to skip first grade, but my parents and I decided against it.

Anyway, I have an older sister, about four years older. She is absolutely beautiful and always has been. My entire life, as I received awards for my knowledge, I listened to her receive praise and attention for her beauty. I was so jealous of her I could taste it.

When I went into sixth grade, I was handed my enrollment papers for the enrichment program that year. When I reported to the room with the other "brains," I took one look around and walked out. I think it was at that moment that I decided I wanted to be more than just a "smart girl with a bright future." I wanted to be the pretty one.

So, that's when it started. I made completely new friends and stopped focusing on my grades. I began drinking when I was thirteen—heavily—and continued until I was nineteen. I didn't get into the schools of my choice because of my grades. I failed out of a decent university after my freshman year. I got involved with horrible guys, bad friends, and even landed myself in a mental hospital for three months.

I don't feel I lost my intelligence that day or over time, I just feel that on that day I made a choice that has led me down some difficult roads.

I am not a whiner and can't truly complain about where I am today. I have a good job, make decent money, and have a great family. But I still wonder every day what would have happened had I stayed in that enrichment program, took my talent more seriously, and had not adopted the lazy attitude I've grown so used to.

I look at my beautiful sister now and I'm not at all jealous of her. Instead, I am jealous of the focused, determined little girl I used to be.

Name withheld, 24, financial retail My only regret in my life concerns my sister. She was in an accident two years before I was born, leaving her mentally and physically handicapped. It also emotionally handicapped my family.

Up until I was twelve years old, I resented the attention she received from my family. I would throw tantrums, sulk, and be an obnoxious brat whenever I was around her. But every time I screamed, cried, or yelled, she would just hold me or rock me, crooning, "Baby, don't cry. Be happy, please."

My sister never went past the age of five, mentally. She was the sweetest, purest, most gentle and loving person I have ever had the chance to be around. What happened when I was twelve that stopped the selfish behaviour was my sister's death.

This is where my regret comes in: I regret never having told her how much I truly did love her; never thanking her for the way she touched my life. I pray that up in heaven she hears me say, "I love you" every night.

But out of all of this came something good: I learned how to love unselfishly.

Susan, 29, sales and marketing I do not regret carelessly. I do not say, "I'm sorry" very easily. In my short lifetime, I have had a variety of self-revelating [sic] experiences, but I am happy to say I do not have a lifetime of regrets. I cannot even think of something I would have done differently if given the chance. I accept the choices I have made and am comfortable with where I am and who I am today. I consider myself lucky—very lucky.

I am certainly not saying I have not made mistakes because I have made plenty, but most I have tried to correct or make up for and, at the very least, learn from them. I do not regret what I have learned and, therefore, I do not regret the mistakes I have made that have led me to grow and learn. I refuse to live in the past and wonder how things could be different.

I have had an abortion and I do not regret it. It was not a mistake; I made the right decision for that time in my life. Later, I had a miscarriage and sometimes I am sad about that, but I cannot regret it. Regrets, I think, are reserved for personal actions or inactions.

A friend and former lover just recently revealed a regret of his that had to do with me, or more specifically, the two of us. I reminded him how I feel about regrets and he asked an interesting question:

"Is it the regret itself that is bad or what you do with it?"

Afterword

It's amazing how profound—how *incredibly* profound—most people can be when given the chance. That's evident from numerous respondents who, by now, should have given you plenty to think about. A man, a woman, or even a teenager, who shook you up, pissed you off, hit you upside the head, or just stopped you cold.

Someone who scared you, shocked you, stimulated, or engaged you.

Someone who made you laugh, made you cry, made you cringe, or made you pause—to reflect.

The goal of RegretsOnly.com from day one has been getting people to reflect upon their lives so that others may learn from their experiences. In doing so, we can learn to appreciate what we can discover about ourselves.

The most significant thing I've discovered from this project is also the simplest: people everywhere just want their voices to he heard. Be it face-to-face, over the telephone, or via the Internet, they want acknowledgment and recognition. They also want to make their mark in this world and leave something indelible behind for future generations. In fact, I'm convinced that is the primary reason people participated in the first place—to be able to say, "That's me! I wrote this and I'm glad I contributed something."

Of course, we may not always *agree* with one another, but whenever I hear the words "Thanks for listening to me," I know it makes a big impact on that person. So on behalf of the 290 courageous individuals who are included here, I want to thank you, the reader, for "listening" to what they had to say.

As a result, perhaps you will be motivated to examine your own life and resolve to do things a little differently from now on. Whether in matters of the heart or the mind, ultimately, the decision rests with you.

If you share a common bond with someone in this book, conceivably his or her experience will influence you in a meaningful way. Maybe not today or tomorrow, but someday, one of these voices may speak loudly to you when you face a similar situation. Or, more accurately, a similar choice.

Regrets are all about choices. And frequently, our choices involve risk, with certain choices undoubtedly riskier than others. To paraphrase Shakespeare, "To act, or not to act: that is the question."

Personally, the opportunities I *didn't* act upon in my life are usually the ones I regretted most: the unshared adventures, the unsaid words, the unwritten articles, the unmet challenges, the unopened doors. It's all this *un*finished business that I always promise myself I will get to—eventually.

So whenever people say their regrets "build character" and have made them the person they are, I couldn't agree more.

But I also think there's an even broader question that needs to be asked: *Exactly what type of person do you hope to be?*

All of which brings to mind a poem I've kept for years. I found it, torn and yellowed, buried deep inside my desk drawer. Fittingly, it was written by an anonymous author and is aptly titled, *The Dilemma*:

To laugh is to risk appearing a fool.

To weep is to risk appearing sentimental.

To reach out for another is to risk involvement.

To expose feelings is to risk rejection.

To place your dreams before the crowd is to risk ridicule.

To love is to risk not being loved in return.

To go forward in the face of overwhelming odds is to risk failure.

But risks must be taken because the greatest hazard in life is to risk nothing. The person who risks nothing, does nothing, has nothing, is nothing.

He may avoid suffering and sorrow, but he cannot learn, feel, change, grow or love. Chained by his certitudes, he is a slave. He has forfeited his freedom.

Only a person who dares to risk is free.

Your comments and suggestions are welcomed.
You can e-mail Barry at: barrycadish@regretsonly.com

To contribute your own regret(s),
please visit www.RegretsOnly.com
Or write to:
Regrets Only
P.O. Box 42
Lake Oswego, OR 97034-0005